IF WE COULD HEAR THEM NOW

ENCOUNTERS WITH LEGENDARY JEWISH HEROINES

IF WE COULD HEAR THEM NOW

ENCOUNTERS WITH LEGENDARY JEWISH HEROINES

ALICE BECKER LEHRER

Alice Beckerlehrer

URIM PUBLICATIONS
Jerusalem • New York

If We Could Hear Them Now:
Encounters with Legendary Jewish Heroines
By Alice Becker Lehrer
Copyright © 2009 by Alice Becker Lehrer

Printed in Israel. First Edition.

ISBN-13: 978-965-524-031-3

URIM FICTION
Urim Publications, P.O. Box 52287, Jerusalem 91521 Israel
Lambda Publishers Inc.
527 Empire Blvd., Brooklyn, New York 11225 U.S.A.
Tel: 718-972-5449 Fax: 718-972-6307, mh@ejudaica.com

www.UrimPublications.com

For my children
and my children's children

There is one who sings the song of his own life,
and in himself he finds everything, his full spiritual sufficiency.

There is another who sings the songs of his people.
He leaves the circle of his private existence,
for he does not find it broad enough.
He aspires for the heights
and he attaches himself with tender love to the whole of Israel,
he sings her songs, grieves in her afflictions,
and delights in her hopes.
He ponders lofty and pure thoughts
concerning her past and her future,
and probes lovingly and wisely the content of her inner essence.

Then there is one whose spirit extends
beyond the boundary of Israel, to sing the song of man....
He is drawn to man's universal vocation
and he hopes for his highest perfection.
And this is the life source from which
he draws his thoughts and probing, his yearnings and his visions.

But there is one who rises even higher,
uniting himself with the whole existence,
with all creatures, with all worlds.
With all of them he sings his song.
It is of one such as this that tradition has said
that whoever sings a portion of song each day
is assured of the life of the world to come.[1]

– Abraham Isaac Kook

---

[1] Kook,Abraham Isaac. *The Lights of Penitence, Lights of Holiness, The Moral Principles, Essays, Letters, and Poems.* Translation and Introduction by Ben Zion Bokser. New Jersey: Paulist Press, 1978, p. 22.

CONTENTS

ACKNOWLEDGMENTS

WE ARE not alone, neither in life nor in any of our endeavors. The products of our lives are never the result of our efforts by themselves. The inspirations or original ideas that come to us are linked to all our experiences. Therefore, in this book, I acknowledge all the elements in my life that have led me to the path that enabled me to see it published.

I was deeply inspired by all the authors of my source material as well as those in my immediate circle of teachers and friends – Rabbi Reuven Poupko for the brilliance and clarity of thought that I so admire, and Rabbi Chaim Steinmetz for his enthusiasm and challenging insights. I am especially thankful that my path has crossed that of Rabbi Dini Lewittes, for whom I feel deep affection and admiration. Rabbi Dini gets me to nudge the envelope. Her imagination and creative thinking are always inspiring, and her courage to think and act out of the box push me to go further in my own efforts.

I am grateful to those who encouraged me with comments, editing, and good criticism: Barbara Sutnick, Joyce Rappaport, and Channah Magori. I valued the opinions of Tova Shimon, Katherine Orloff, and Betty Palik Prupas very much.

I thank Tzvi Mauer of Urim Publications. I thank my editor, Rahel Jaskow, for her guidance; her knowledge and skills enhanced all that I did. I also thank Michal Alatin for her assistance.

Monique Polak's words – "Don't give up!" – always reverberated within me at the right time. I came away from each encounter with her more charged and focused than ever. Her vibrant enthusiasm for the creative endeavour is contagious.

I shared some material with Linda Adams Troy, Rona Davis, Randi Zittrer, Terry Trager, Lilianne Aberman, Robin Mader, Barbara Segal, and Martha Miller, all of whose comments were of great value. Randi also assisted me very much by doing detailed research, for which I am grateful.

Gil Troy has been not only a mentor but also a compassionate courier of the manuscript. Always there to guide me through the publishing world, he does so happily and with encouragement, as if there were no other demands upon his busy life. The opinions and guidance of Linda and Gil are precious to me. I am honored to be their friend and Linda's *havruta*. Geographical distance – measured in oceans and thousands of miles – has not been an obstacle to our weekly study sessions.

My mother, Henriette Reutlinger Becker and my late father, Sidney Joshua Becker, endowed me with what it has taken to reach this point in life. I am eternally thankful to them, and I enjoy seeing my mother experience pride and joy in me and all of her thriving extended family.

My daughters, Michelle Lehrer and Angela Lehrer Vineberg, are the jewels of my life. We keep each other up to date with what is relevant in today's world and in our Jewish heritage. They inspired me to bring new life to the Jewish heroines in this book in the hope that they might keep them alive in their busy lives. I write for them, for Michael Vineberg, my son-in-law, and for my two precious grandsons, Jacob and Benjamin. Neville Eisenberg, Michelle's dear friend, has had a "title" role in this book as well, and I thank him.

I leave for last the most cherished muse in my life, my husband, Harold Lehrer. My true other half, he has always been the one who is most supportive of my endeavors. Harold knows that "I have been fearful in the midst of my joy… and have rejoiced in the midst of my fear. And my love has surpassed them both" (King David).

INTRODUCTION

I HAVE always been obsessed with leaders and heroes – those who were out of the ordinary, whose lives changed direction because they dared to do something unusual either in a single instant or over time. To me, a hero is anyone who opens the door not merely wide enough for him/herself to pass through, but also holds it open for others. At various times in our lives, we are all on the verge of being heroes, even for only a moment. Yet mostly, we resist the urge to extend the hand, make the statement, or even think the thought that might transform us. Normalcy is not visionary. Its appetite stops at satisfaction.[1] Nevertheless, it is perfectly all right to be ordinary. It is decent and dutiful, conventional and lawful. But to be extraordinary is to be altruistic, to reach out in *hesed*, to go beyond the letter of the law. It means being exceptional and gutsy. And while we may not all be heroes, we can visit their lives and be enriched by them.

Heroes' lives, which also contain a timeless element, become gifts of lessons for our own lives. When we learn about past heroes, "the hour is transformed into infinity, the moment into eternity... the fleeting, evanescent moment is transformed into eternity."[2] Heroes also know that we are judged not only by our thoughts, but also by our speech and our actions. They survive the judgment of others and move into prominence because they exemplify service for the sake of the greater good.

I wished to emphasize the timelessness of the lives of the heroines I have chosen to include in this book. I hope that I have brought it from the shelves of libraries and study halls to the reader.

---

[1] *Megillat Ruth: Hesed and Hutzpah, A Literary Approach.* Study Guide by Noam Zion. Shalom Hartman Institute, Jerusalem. 2005.

[2] Soloveitchik, Rabbi Joseph B. *Halachic Man.* Philadelphia: JPS, 1984, 118–119.

I chose the heroines in this book simply because I find their stories appealing. I could easily hear them tell their stories today. While some are well-known, others are less so. Although there are many others whose stories are of equal appeal, my hope is that for now, the women chosen will bring meaning and some added value to the reader's life.

These heroines were all doers. They were not content to talk among themselves or complain about their situations. Some acted on a creative impulse that sprung from within themselves, while others were pushed by circumstance into the roles that they assumed. Each of them showed conviction to the values of truth, justice, and mercy, and dared to believe in a God Who sought out humankind as a partner in nurturing these values in the world. They experienced a moment of truth, in some cases sudden and in others gradual, but knew in that defining moment that what is true for one is good for all.[3]

I have allowed the heroines of this book to tell their stories as though they were answering an interviewer's questions. Since questions are the basis of Jewish learning, I felt them to be an important element in the book. While I have fictionalized the heroines' stories somewhat, they remain closely tied to the Tanach and in some cases to the Midrash, so that what they say here is plausible and in character.

All the women in this book offer us the relevance of their life stories for today. Some hid their Jewish identity only to proclaim it openly later on, while others, who thought themselves ordinary at first, responded to the needs of the time and took responsibility for fulfilling that need for the greater good. Some, who excelled in their Jewish knowledge and leadership, could have been leaders today. Others showed remarkable courage in the face of terrible danger. All of them are heroes of Jewish survival.

---

[3] Sarah Yehudit Schneider, www.astillsmallvoice.org.

Let these heroines remind us to follow them, even by taking baby steps, toward a better world. Perhaps our own generation can influence future generations in their choice of heroes.

TAMAR

TAMAR'S STORY is an important one in Jewish history as it reflects the common experience of intermarriage. But her story is often ignored because of the extraordinary disguise that she, the outsider, used in order to lure Judah back to his roots and responsibilities.

Tamar's story is about the courage to use unconventional means to prove that individuals who make up a community are responsible for each other. This is what makes Tamar a hero. Just as heroes are unconventional, so is she. Just as she did not need Judah's compensation but rather his commitment, we do not need material affirmation as much as we need healthy emotional connections with each other.[1]

After arranging the sale of his brother Joseph to a caravan of Midianite traders, Judah fled his family and his land to live among the Canaanites. Although he was not the firstborn, he had been the leader among his eleven brothers, who eventually would form the twelve tribes of Israel. But jealousy and anger had clouded his judgment, making him forget the values and ethics he had been taught by his father Jacob, the third Patriarch in Jewish history.

In his new life, Judah married a non-Jewish woman with whom he had three sons. He chose a local woman, Tamar, as a wife for the eldest, Er. When Er died unexpectedly, Tamar was married by levirate custom[2] to Onan, the middle son. When Onan died, also unexpectedly, Judah promised Tamar that he would marry her to

---

[1] From a shiur given by Rabbi Chaim Steinmetz on Parashat Vayeshev, Kollel Torah Mitzion, Montreal, December, 2002.

[2] Levirate marriage: "The Torah provides that if a husband dies childless, his widow and brother should marry. In case the brother does not wish to go through with the marriage, there is a process known as *chalitzah*, which severs the bond between them" (*The Stone Edition Chumash*, 1063). This obligation could be extended to other relatives, as Judah did later in the narrative. Today, only the ritual of *chalitzah* is performed.

his youngest son, Shelah, as soon as Shelah became old enough to marry – thus keeping her in the family – and asked her to wait until then. Tamar agreed, not knowing that Judah, who feared that Shelah would die too, had no intention of keeping his promise to her.

Shortly afterwards, Judah's own wife died. After the mourning period was over, Judah went to the local sheep-shearing festival. Knowing this, Tamar disguised herself as a prostitute in order to encounter him, thus imposing a commitment to marry her and fulfill his promise not to cast her aside.

"We should not be scandalized by Tamar's actions, because we know her reasons."[3] Unlike other religions and cultures, Judaism accepts that "the two qualities of sexuality and intense spirituality are not mutually exclusive."[4] Tamar is a model of integrity and commitment.

According to one interpretation of Tamar's story, the non-Jewish partner sees the merit of Jewish traditions more clearly that the Jewish partner does. Tamar seems to understand the value of Jewish tradition more than Judah himself does, and also sees that Jewish identity is in danger of being cast away by Jews themselves.

Tamar makes us question whether we, too, have laid our Judaism aside at times because of our personal experiences. Her story leads us to ask whether we, too, have made personal Jewish memory a metaphor for Judaism as a whole and base our commitment solely on our own experience.

Tamar's story is also about the Jew who awakens to understand his responsibilities. Her husband Judah stands as a crucial but threatened link between Judaism's first family and its future. Tamar is the spark that transforms him and thus transforms history,

---

[3] Frymer-Kensky, Tikva. *Reading the Women of the Bible*. New York: Schocken Books, 2002, 269.

[4] Frankiel, Tamar. *The Voice of Sarah*. San Francisco: Harper, 1990, 23.

proving that one person can change history. "Judah was inattentive in his own deep despair. Tamar saw the bigger picture."[5]

When Judah recognizes the righteousness of Tamar's unconventional act, he undergoes a profound inner change. His courage in overcoming his injured pride transforms him into a model of *kiddush ha-Shem* – one who honors God in public by behaving in the highest ethical and moral manner. At this point Judah, "vulnerable, dynamic, responsive with all his being, becomes the paradigm of responsibility and leadership."[6] Together they return to his family of origin, where Judah repairs the rifts between himself and his father and brothers and becomes a responsible and righteous leader.

It is said that we are praised not just for our acts but for our orientation in life. "Strong connections give us visions to reconstruct a family that was broken. Tamar steps into the realm of her personal power through her sexuality... and her strategy was a righteous one." It is "not about sexual freedom, but acting rightly from the essential being as a woman."[7] "By continuing to consider herself a member of Judah's family and insisting on securing her own future within it, that family thrived and developed into a dynasty and eventually the Judean state."[8]

Q: WELCOME, TAMAR. Why is your story not often told? Why is it not a usual part of the curriculum in Jewish schools?

Tamar: Many rabbis ignored my story because it is quite risqué. Who would expect a rabbi to relate how a Canaanite woman disguised herself as a prostitute and became pregnant by Judah in order to force him to marry her? Some sages were troubled by that entire incident, and no wonder!

---

[5] Gottlieb Zornberg, Avivah. *Genesis: The Beginning of Desire*. New York: Doubleday, 1995, 327.

[6] *Ibid.,* 328.

[7] Frankiel, Tamar. *The Voice of Sarah*. San Francisco: Harper, 1990, 25, 27.

[8] *Reading the Women of the Bible,* 274.

While Judaism doesn't deny sexuality as part of human nature, the rabbis were afraid that young girls and boys would focus more on the *what* and the *how* of my story and less on the *why*. They feared that students might think prostitution acceptable, which would miss the entire point. My story is more about keeping one's eye on the mark than about the specific method by which one achieves success. Nevertheless, despite some other's finer sensibilities, my story and I are still part of the Torah.

Q: They say that everything about life is included in the Torah.

Tamar: While that is true, I can understand why the sages acted as they did. When the kingdom of Israel was destroyed early in the Common Era, they were responsible for ensuring the Torah's survival. They had to struggle to keep the values of Judaism alive as Jews fled to foreign lands. The oral tradition was what kept Torah alive at that time. Most Jewish values were passed down to the later generations by the women, who practiced them at home as they raised their children. Such ideas as prostitution, intrigue and incest were too much to deal with during those difficult times. So I understand why the focus was on less controversial and provocative stories than mine.

Q: And yet, centuries later, you inspired Esther, who saved the Jews of Persia and paved the way for the rebuilding of the Second Temple in Jerusalem. Maybe the rabbis could not silence you after all! Please tell us more about yourself.

Tamar: I lived in approximately 1500 B.C.E., the biblical era, when the Patriarch Jacob and his clan were all the Hebrews who existed at that time. I lived in Canaan, where my father was a spiritual leader, a priest. My mother was devout, loyal, and warm, and brought me up to respect God and man. We were monotheists but not Hebrews. There were many families like ours.

Q: Like Tzipora, Moses's wife, who was a monotheist, although not a Hebrew. She appeared long after you in history.

Tamar: A quiet, studious, and obedient girl, I spent most of my time by myself and was too quiet for my parents' liking. They believed that if they arranged a marriage for me, I wouldn't be alone as an adult. Arranged marriages were customary then.

Q: Matchmaking among Jews is still alive and well today. Today the matchmaker is often a computer. It works in many cases.

Tamar: Wonderful! I'm the first to say: whatever works!

I inherited a strong spiritual side from my father. Also, I had always dreamed of being a mother. My father, a learned man, had great respect for the Hebrews and their courage to establish a new and noble belief system. He often recounted the stories of the Hebrew founding fathers and mothers and the effect that they had on society. The women in particular intrigued me. I felt a connection to them that I couldn't explain.

We Canaanites lived by the Noahide laws[9] and the Hebrews respected us for that. But the Hebrews took monotheism one step further. They based everything on a single God who loved humankind. They believed that the world had been created in love, justice, and compassion. They believed that human beings are God's partners in perfecting the world. I loved these ideas.

Jacob and his children were the Hebrews of my generation. One of Jacob's sons, Judah, married a local woman when he moved away from his family, and they had three sons. When I was married to the oldest of them, Er, Judah became my father-in-law.

Q: It would seem that Judah wandered far from his roots.

Tamar: He did – and as fate would have it, he found his way to my community.

---

[9] The seven Noahide laws, which apply to all humanity, are: 1) not to deny God, 2) not to blaspheme God, 3) not to commit murder, 4) not to engage in illicit sexual relationships, 5) not to steal, 6) not to eat a limb from a living animal, and 7) to set up courts to ensure obedience to the other six laws. According to Rabbi Joseph Telushkin, "These laws constitute the standard by which Jews assess the morality of a non-Jewish society" (*Jewish Literacy*. New York: William Morrow & Company, 1991, 509).

Judah was the fourth son of Jacob and Leah, who had named him in praise of God, grateful to have borne yet another fine, strong son. Commanding and charismatic, he was a leader among his brothers.[10]

But he also had an insatiable hunger for his father's approval. Although he wanted to be the favored son, he could not compete with Joseph, the son of Rachel, the only one of Jacob's wives whom he truly loved.[11] Joseph was also exceptionally handsome. Jacob loved him best.[12] This haunted Judah, and he struggled a great deal because of it. His natural charm and charisma usually kept him out of trouble, but not always.

Q: What do you mean?

Tamar: Joseph was a constant thorn in his brothers' side, reminding them of his special bond with their father Jacob. The brothers, who were terribly upset by Jacob's favoritism, even feared that they would lose their inheritances to Joseph.

The sibling rivalry was strongest between Joseph, who was Jacob's favorite, and Judah, who was the brothers' natural leader. The brothers followed Judah in whatever he said, including in what started out as a plan to be rid of Joseph forever. Yet it was Judah's leadership and sense of responsibility that saved Joseph's life in the end, and saved Jacob's sons from repeating the first murder committed in the Bible: that of Adam's son Abel, who was killed by his own brother, Cain.[13]

Q: As an aside, this could well be a lesson in child-rearing – not to indulge in favoritism.

---

[10] Judah was known as a "man of extraordinary physical strength as well as an eloquent and persuasive speaker, [who] wield[ed] considerable influence both within the family and in the family's relations with the outside world" (*Chronicles: News of the Past*, vol. 1, no. 5. Jerusalem: Reubeni Foundation, 1958).

[11] Genesis 29:18, 20.

[12] Genesis 37:3–4.

[13] Genesis 4:1–16.

Tamar: Exactly. It is an extremely important lesson in the Torah, which is full of examples of life's situations. Jacob's early parenting methods are an excellent demonstration of what not to do.

When Judah led his brothers in their plan to dispose of Joseph, he became an example of charisma turned into corruption and of abuse of power. Judah had power over his brothers, but instead of using it for good, he succumbed to personal envy.

Q: It seems that we are all vulnerable to our leaders' personal motives.

Tamar: Exceptional people are examples of the human struggle for goals that are either for the greater good or for personal gain. The better of the two is ultimately the one who is judged favorably.

Judah's plan stemmed from personal motives. When Joseph approached the brothers' encampment, where his father Jacob had sent him, he led his brothers in seizing Joseph and throwing him into a pit that, at least according to one report, was full of snakes and scorpions.[14] I believe that, like Reuven, he intended to pull him out later, once the brothers felt that he'd suffered enough. But I think that he quickly realized that it would be impossible. By that time, things had gone too far.

Q: Are you saying that the brothers had not intended to kill Joseph at first, even though they said explicitly that they wanted to?

Tamar: When people are angry, they say all kinds of wild things that they don't really mean. And since the brothers were furious with Joseph, it's no wonder that they talked about killing him the moment they laid eyes on him. But when Reuven suggested that they throw him alive into the pit instead of murdering him, they agreed right away. They could have refused and gone on with their plan – after all, they outnumbered Reuven substantially! But they didn't. They let Joseph live. So my answer to your question is no, I don't think that they meant to kill him at first. I think that all they

---

14 Rashi on Genesis 37:24.

21

wanted to do was to take their anger out on him, make him suffer and beg them for mercy. Yet paradoxically, it was this momentary impulse of mercy that put Joseph in more danger than ever.

Q: How so?

Tamar: It takes a leader to see all facets of a situation, and Judah, the natural leader among his brothers, now realized where things were headed. If the brothers took Joseph out of the pit and brought him back home, even if they intimidated him into keeping silent or swore him to secrecy, he would still have a powerful hold over them. Under these circumstances, he was no longer a mere annoyance but an actual threat, and this they would not tolerate. Therefore, there was no longer any way that he could live among them in safety, even if Judah and Reuven managed to get him home alive.

Q: So the appearance of the Ishmaelite caravan[15] was a lucky turn of events for your future brother-in-law.

Tamar: I think that Judah saw it as nothing less than a miracle.

Q: We can't forget that Judah was about to sell his own brother into slavery – a dreadful fate, particularly in that time and place. The fact that Joseph was fortunate later on doesn't excuse what Judah did.

Tamar: I don't excuse Judah's part in the affair. But in this specific situation, I believe he saw that caravan as Joseph's last chance for survival.

Q: Nevertheless, the brothers' actions – the assault and subsequent enslavement of their own kin, together with the heinous deception of their father, would be recognized as crimes in any age – crimes that cried out for justice.

---

[15] Genesis 37:21–36.

Tamar: Of course. Judah understood this, and his conscience was far from clear. Soon afterwards, he left his family and came to live among us in Timna.

Q: How did your fellow townspeople feel about Judah's arrival?

Tamar: All of Timna was abuzz with gossip. Rumors flew about why Judah had left such a well-known and well-established family. His close friend and business partner, Hirah, lived in our neighborhood. That is how my family came to know Judah.

Q: So it was here that he married Bat Shua and became the father of Er, Onan and Shelah?

Tamar: Yes. Judah changed dramatically once he came to our community. He thought he could run away from his past with all of its sadness, guilt, unresolved anger, and disappointment in himself. So he dealt with it by doing what many people do. He married out of his faith and quickly had children in order to start a new life. His family of origin had always chosen their wives carefully to ensure that their values and traditions would remain strong. But Judah rebelled. He removed himself as the next link in the chain.

Q: Surely you are not suggesting that marrying out of one's faith is necessarily an act of anger or rebellion.

Tamar: No, not always, but sometimes it can be.

Q: There are many variables in intermarriage. In modern times, children live fully in the non-Jewish world. It is hard not to assimilate.

Tamar: That was true in our day as well.

I was married to Judah's son Er, who died soon after the wedding. I was upset but not distraught, since there had been no physical or emotional intimacy in our relationship.

According to the tradition at the time, I was obliged to marry Judah's next oldest son, Onan, in order to carry over Er's title of inheritance as the firstborn. This was known as a levirate marriage, whose purpose was to keep the family line intact.[16] Judah maintained some Jewish values, and this was one of them. So I married Onan willingly. I was happy to help Judah keep at least one of his traditions.

But my marriage to Onan turned out to be as disastrous as my marriage to Er had been. He, too, died unexpectedly soon after our wedding. Since I had not had a child by either brother, I was alone once more. Although I did not know it at the time, Judah suspected that I had somehow caused their deaths.[17] He committed that he would marry me to his third and youngest son, Shelah, when he came of age, but in the meantime, he sent me back to my father's home.

Q: You must have felt terrible.

Tamar: I did. To make matters worse, Judah did not send for me when Shelah came of age. I continued to wait, thinking that perhaps Judah wanted to keep his last surviving son by his side for a little while longer, but eventually I realized that he had no intention of keeping his promise. It seemed that my dream of one day becoming a mother would never come true. There was only one thing I could do to ensure my future – conceive a child by him. It was my right, and I had to hold Judah to his promise that I would marry into his family. I had only to wait for the right time and place.

Q: Waiting is difficult, isn't it?

Tamar: Oh, yes! It's very difficult to be patient, but patience is rewarded in time. Suddenly, Judah's wife died, leaving him free to marry. I began to work out my strategy. To Judah, either I didn't exist or he simply was avoiding me, blaming me for his sons'

---

[16] Levirate marriage was a way of preserving the "sublime moral dignity of the family, to continue the human race in the direction set by the traits predominating in that family." *The Pentateuch: Translation and Excerpts from the Commentary of Samson Raphael Hirsch.* New York: The Judaica Press, 1986, 168.
[17] Rashi on Genesis 38:11.

deaths.[18] Death disturbed his conscience and reminded him of his brother Joseph. At this point, he had no idea that I could bring new meaning to his life. He did not realize that I could redeem him, his family, and even the future of the Jewish people.[19]

I realized that the only way to accomplish my goal was to seduce Judah without letting him know who I was. After all, if Jacob had spent his wedding night with Leah thinking that she was Rachel, perhaps the same thing could work with me. If I became pregnant, then Judah would marry me.

Q: You were quite the girl, different from what people must have assumed.

Tamar: I *was* different. And I was determined – and lucky, too. Just when the time was ripe in my monthly cycle, I received word that Judah, whose mourning time was over, would be going up to the sheep-shearing festival. So I washed and anointed myself, and then I slipped out of my house wearing colorful veils and wraps under my plain widow's dress. I went to the crossroads near the spring, where I knew that Judah would be passing by, took off my plain clothing and sat in my colorful robes, dressed as a prostitute, keeping careful watch on the road. When I saw Judah approaching, I veiled my face and stood up. The coins decorating my veils jingled, whispering my presence to his loneliness. I bent to let the veils around my ankles loose, and they wrapped around his. I welcomed him into the night and saw his wanting. He was terribly eager and begged me to let him *consort* with me – I'm not sure what the word for this is today. But I have to admit that my scheme worked. About thirty-five hundred years ago, this was one way that unmarried men and women could meet unaccompanied.

Q: Prostitution still exists today.

---

[18] Rashi on Genesis 38:11.

[19] The lineage of Tamar and Judah gives rise to the Davidic line of Jewish kingship, from which it is believed the Messiah will come.

Tamar: Yes, indeed it does. Back then, though, there were two main kinds of prostitutes. There was the *kadeshah,* the ritual prostitute, with whom men had encounters as part of the local religion, and there was the *zonah,* the ordinary prostitute, who worked for pay, just like today. Judah thought I was the latter kind, but I don't think it made much difference to him either way. All he wanted was someone to comfort him in his loneliness.

In any case, when I asked Judah what he would pay me, he offered to send me a young goat from his flock once he got back home. Since he didn't have a young goat with him at the time – as I knew he would not – we agreed that he would give me something valuable as collateral. So far everything was going exactly according to plan, and I was so excited! I didn't care about the payment, of course. What I wanted was something that would identify Judah specifically, something that would serve as proof that we had been together. I asked him for his seal-ring, his cloak and his walking stick, and in the heat of the moment, he handed them to me. I put them away in my bundle, taking care to hide my excitement. I had to keep up my disguise, pretend that I was all business, but at the same time I could hardly believe that my plan had succeeded so well!

When our encounter had been consummated, I slipped away, put my plain robe back on and ran home. For weeks, I could think of nothing else but what had happened between us. After having been so close to Judah, I knew for certain that he had the potential to become a sensitive husband and a great leader.

When Judah came back home from the sheep-shearing festival, he chose a young goat and asked his friend Hirah to take it to me at the crossroads near the spring. He wanted to get back his ring, cloak and walking stick, but of course I wasn't there. Hirah asked the locals where he could find the prostitute who worked at the crossroads, but they knew nothing, since I had never been there before that day and never went back. So Judah let his ring, cloak and walking stick go as quietly and surely as he had dismissed me from his life.

Q: And then you discovered that you were pregnant.

Tamar: Yes, either by coincidence or by a miracle. My parents were horrified at first, but eventually they understood my plan to right a wrong, to become a mother, to lead a man back to his roots where he could grow into a leader of his people. They helped me see my plan through.

Q: And so the story unfolds....

Tamar: It does have its element of suspense. When Judah found out that I, his disastrous daughter-in-law, had gone and gotten myself pregnant out of wedlock, he wanted to have me burned at the stake. I suspect that he also thought it would be a convenient way to get rid of me once and for all. But then, quietly, through his messenger, I sent him the things that he had left with me – his ring, cloak and staff – together with a message that the owner of those items was the man who had made me pregnant. I held my breath for what seemed an eternity until Judah realized that he had to face his moment of truth. He had to take responsibility for his actions, which he had avoided doing until now. He realized that he had neglected his obligation of levirate marriage until I forced him to fulfill it. I believe he also saw a vision of himself as being no one at all, having fallen far from his roots.

Q: You took quite a risk, Tamar. You were lucky that Judah had a moment of truth.

Tamar: Indeed I was – and so was the Jewish people. When Judah saw his own possessions and realized that I was the one who had seduced him and was now carrying his child – actually, children, as it turned out later on – he relived all his losses. He remembered the day that he had held Joseph's bloodied coat up to his father, claiming that Joseph had been killed by a wild animal. In the blink of an eye, a *rega,* an instant, he could repair his life, begin his journey of reconciliation, and return home. He realized that I was his second chance in life.

In front of all the assembled people, he announced, *"Tzadkah mimeni* – she is more righteous than I."[20] The rest of our story was a beautiful reconciliation with his father and brothers back home.

Q: It seems that persistence to hold on to your dream played an important part.

Tamar: Yes, though it wasn't easy. Still, in a single moment, every one of us has what it takes to change things.

Q: And create happy endings.

Tamar: Indeed. Judah took back his responsibility as a leader among his brothers, eventually finding Joseph in Egypt and reconciling with him. It's a suspenseful and emotional story, a good read in the Torah.[21]

I gave birth to twin boys whom Judah named Peretz and Zerah, meaning "strength" and "brightness." My sons loved each other and thrived, and they were the first brothers in Jewish history to have a peaceful relationship. At their birth, the word *hineh* – "behold" – was repeated several times, which usually signals a significant event in the Bible. And so it was, because my son Peretz became the ancestor of David, King of Israel, the epitome of faith, knowledge, strength and humility. It was David who established the Jews in the city of Jerusalem as a sovereign nation, and it was in Jerusalem that the first great Temple was built by David's son, Solomon.

Q: How proud you must be.

Tamar: Of acting the prostitute? No. But unconventional means may sometimes justify the ends if they are used for the sake of Heaven, especially if no harm is done, no other opportunity exists, and there is no pleasure or gain in such an act. And if I could change the world, then anyone can. I am so glad that in modern times I can tell my story freely.

---

[20] Genesis 38:26.
[21] Genesis 42–45.

Q: So are we all! Thank you, Tamar.

SERAH BAT ASHER

A LEGEND of Jewish history, Serah bat Asher was the longest-living Jew during the Jewish exile in Egypt. She held all her people's secrets from the past and knew the signs that would show that the time for liberation had arrived.

After significant events occurred in the Bible, a census was often taken in order to learn how many Jews survived. Serah bat Asher is named in two censuses in the Torah that were taken three hundred and fifty years apart, which would make her a very old lady indeed at the time of the second census. Other than this, the Bible tells us nothing of her.

The first time that Serah's name appears is when she is listed as Asher's daughter and as one of the seventy people in Jacob's family who went to Egypt in order to escape the famine in Canaan.[1] This journey took place in approximately 1750 B.C.E. The second mention of Serah bat Asher is in a census of the Jews taken three hundred and fifty years later, in approximately 1400 B.C.E., after the liberation from Egypt.[2]

"In the Bible, Serah has only a name, but in Midrash (rabbinic lore), she has a powerful myth attached to her; Serah is the personification of wisdom and the link among generations."[3] Because there is no narrative about Serah, her life is a puzzle. If she lived for more than three hundred and fifty years, the Midrash created the pieces of the puzzle as follows:

Serah, a granddaughter of Jacob, was born in Canaan. It is likely that she was named after Abraham's wife, her great-great-grandmother Sarah. Her father, Asher, who was one of Jacob's

---

[1] Genesis 46:17.

[2] Numbers 26:46.

[3] Hammer, Jill. *Sisters at Sinai*. Philadelphia: The Jewish Publication Society, 2004, 267.

twelve sons and the leader of one of the twelve tribes of Israel, was known for reconciling family disputes.[4] His tribe's symbol was an olive tree on a background of gold. The olive branch, which is bitter, became a symbol of reconciliation between God and humanity after the Flood, in Noah's time. Better to eat bitter food in freedom, blessed by God's Providence, than delicacies under the domination of human beings alone.[5]

Serah, too, was a reconciler. She brought the knowledge of the past to validate the present and to start the Jews on their journey toward their future. The Passover story is one of Judaism's most significant texts on this narrative of Jewish exile and liberation, but the legend of Serah bat Asher in that narrative remains untold. Here, she tells us her story.

Q: WELCOME, Serah. Please bring your story to light for us.

Serah: As you now know, I lived to be a very old lady. My grandfather Jacob had blessed me with long life, and little did I know it would come true. In a life that spanned several generations, I became a link for the Jews to their past. I was the only Jew who had gone down to Egypt with my grandfather, his sons, and all their families, and I was the only one of all of them who lived to see the Exodus.

When Grandfather Jacob blessed me with long life, he also gave me certain secrets to keep until the liberation. He told me that although the Israelites would try several times to leave Egypt, I would know when the time was right and I would be instrumental in recognizing the real leader to freedom. At the time, I thought that my grandfather had merely been expressing his love and gratitude. I didn't realize that he had given me a blessing that would actually come true.

---

[4] *Chronicles – News of the Past, in the Days of the Bible,* vol. 5, 2.

[5] *BT Eruvin* 18b. *Perek Shira,* 69: "Master of the Universe, may my food be as bitter as an olive but dependent upon You, rather than sweet as honey but dependent on flesh and blood."

Q: How did you merit his confidence?

Serah: My grandfather knew that we were headed for a long, harsh exile in which Jewish memory might easily fade into distant shadows of the past. He also recognized how critical timing and conditions would be to our liberation. He needed to transfer his prophecy to someone who knew how to respect the past. I remembered everything about each member of our family with perfect clarity, wrote songs about them and sang them with my harp. When my grandfather heard these songs, he realized that I was a keeper of things that would otherwise have been forgotten. He was a brilliant strategist. When he realized that he could rely upon me as the repository of our collective memory, he entrusted me with the secrets of a nation.

Q: Jacob seemed to know you very well.

Serah: My grandfather had spent twenty-two years mourning for Joseph, his favorite son. During that time, I visited him frequently to comfort him with my music. When he was told that Joseph had died, part of his own spirit died as well. I still remember how pale he was when he told us, "I will go down to the grave mourning for my son."[6]

I was determined not to let that happen. Maybe I couldn't prevent what had happened to poor Uncle Joseph, but I could still do everything I could to make certain that Grandfather would not die of grief. My music nurtured his spirit and became an oasis of peace and tranquility for him. He would eat only after I sang to him. Throughout all the years that I played and sang for him, Grandfather Jacob saw and heard and understood how deeply I cherished the family history.

When the terrible famine struck Canaan and my uncles went to Egypt to buy food, they discovered that my uncle Joseph was not only alive, but that he was second only to Pharaoh himself and in charge of all the food in Egypt! The news shook our family. Of

---

6 Genesis 38:35.

course we had to tell Grandfather Jacob, but by then he was elderly and frail and we feared that the news might kill him. As the family was debating how to tell him, my father and uncles saw me in the shadows and realized that I would be the perfect messenger. They trusted me to relay this strange turn of events gently and without shock through my music.[7]

Q: Did you agree to tell him?

Serah: Of course! I cherished being the soft voice that had sustained him in his unhappiness. I approached him, playing my harp and singing to his heart – a simple ballad about a father reunited with his lost son. Then my uncles came in and gave him proof that Joseph was alive. To our relief, instead of fainting, Jacob's spirit was instantly renewed. He sat upright for the first time in many years and insisted on going to see Joseph immediately. I will never forget the joy in his voice when he said, "My son Joseph is alive! I will go and see him before I die."[8]

Q: So you and your family went to Egypt to escape the famine and be reunited with Joseph. But why did you settle in Goshen rather than the capital where Joseph lived?

Serah: Uncle Joseph told Pharaoh and his people that since we were shepherds, we would settle in Goshen so as not to offend the Egyptians, who looked down on the profession. We were a group of refugees who had crossed their border, and my uncle wanted to show the Egyptians that we would contribute to their society and not be a burden. He also realized that if we had our own land to settle on, we would be able keep our own customs and lifestyle. In this way, my uncle protected us. We were grateful.

Q: This relates to events today, in which many countries struggle with an influx of immigrants and their mosaics of customs. Throughout history, Jews have eased into their host countries and

---

[7] Zornberg, 281.

[8] *Genesis* 45:28.

become contributors to the local economy. Would you say that the Goshen model is a good one?

Serah: Yes, I think I would. Life in Goshen was good, for us and for the Egyptians. I married a wonderful young man, and we raised a family. Often, we visited my uncle or he visited us. My uncle was very handsome, you know, and he was also beautiful on the inside. He took us to meet Pharaoh, which was thrilling but a little frightening, too. After all, Pharaoh was a dictator. Most pharaohs of Egypt were cruel and oppressive, but luckily for us, this pharaoh was a wise ruler and kind to his subjects. When Grandfather died, Pharaoh permitted my father and all my uncles, including Uncle Joseph, whom he needed so much to help him run his kingdom, to take his body back to Canaan for burial, which was my grandfather's last wish.[9]

Q: When did life begin to change for the Israelites?

Serah: It happened slowly. For the first few generations after Uncle Joseph died, everything was all right, but then "a new king arose over Egypt who did not know Joseph."[10]

Q: What does that mean, exactly?

Serah: He didn't care who Uncle Joseph had been or what he had done for Egypt, or that we were his family. Instead, he singled us out and blamed us for everything that was wrong with the country, including his own weakness as a ruler.

Q: It sounds similar to what happened to our people many centuries later in a place called Europe, far to the north of Canaan and Egypt.

Serah: During this bitter time, I played and sang to the new generation, keeping hope alive amid hardship. Jacob had blessed me

---

[9] Genesis 50:6.
[10] Exodus 1:8.

34

with a long life so that I would be able to keep the spirit of the Jews alive as they endured their suffering in Egypt.[11]

Q: What was the hope that you clung to?

Serah: To go back to Canaan as free people. We had stayed in Egypt too long.

Q: How did you know when it would be time for the Israelites to go free?

Serah: Before Jacob died, he shared his visions with Uncle Joseph and with me, and told us how we would develop as a nation.[12] He also told Joseph that when the time for our liberation came, I would still be alive, and I would be the only one able to recognize the leader who would liberate us. Later on, when Uncle Joseph was dying, he gathered my uncles and me around his bed: First he made them promise to carry his bones out of Egypt when we left and bury them in Canaan. Then he told me to listen for two words – *pakod yifkod* – which mean "surely remember," because the leader who would eventually liberate us from slavery would use those very words.

Q: What is the significance of the phrase *pakod yifkod?*

Serah: It links us with the promise that God made to my great-great-grandfather Abraham – that eventually we, his descendants, would live as a free nation in our own land, and that God would fulfill His promise to us. The leader whom we were waiting for would know the significance of this phrase, and would utter it. Grandfather Jacob mentioned it in order to remind Joseph of God's promise, and Joseph told me to listen for it as well, since it would mean that our true liberator had arrived. Only a leader who

---

[11] Baskin, Judith R. *Jewish Women in Historical Perspective.* Detroit: Wayne State University Press, 1998, 185.

[12] Weissman, Rabbi Moshe. *The Midrash Says.* New York: Benei Yakov Publications, 1980, 446–447.

knew our history well would know about God's promise to us and use that phrase.

As Uncle Joseph lay dying, he said, "God will surely remember you as a people and bring you out of this land." He used the words in that sentence. Then he linked the land of Canaan to Abraham, Isaac and Jacob, as God had promised it to them and their heirs. Finally, Uncle Joseph repeated it a third time in connection with our solemn promise to take his bones out of Egypt when we eventually left.[13]

When Uncle Joseph died, I mourned together with the rest of the family, and hid my fear of having to carry all our memories by myself. I watched as Joseph's casket was lowered into the river. At that time, who could possibly know that many years later, Moses's mother would set Moses afloat in his basket at that very spot? This is how God harmonizes the notes of every soul of Israel. Coincidences may also be a plan waiting for us.[14]

Q: Yet the Bible says nothing about your role in confirming Moses as the Israelites' liberator.

Serah: I was working behind the scenes. Other people tried to lead us out of Egypt, but failed.[15] When Moses came to us, the elders brought him to see me and asked me whether they could believe Moses. We asked Moses to describe his mission to us, and as he did, I heard him utter that same phrase, *pakod yifkod,* as he told the Israelites to have faith and courage. That was when I knew. I nodded, and that was that.

But there was another condition for leaving. We had to keep our promise to Joseph to take his bones back to Canaan for reburial. Since I was the only living witness who knew his burial

---

13 Genesis 50:24–25.

14 Bialik, Hayyim Nahman, and Ravnitzky, Yehoshua Hanna. *The Book of Legends.* New York: Schocken Books, 1992, 70.

15 Saks, Ilana Goldstein. "Devar Torah for Pesah" (on the Tosafot on BT *Sotah* 13a). Mailed by JOFA (the Jewish Orthodox Feminist Alliance) to its members for Passover 2003.

place, I took our leaders there and they brought up his coffin. This generation had prayed more than any other before them, and Moses was their reward. Now they were ready to become a nation.

Q: The Torah mentions you as the only one to enter Egypt, survive for generations, and live to see the Exodus. Did you also know Miriam, Moses's sister, and Tzipora, his wife?

Serah: I didn't know Moses's wife, Tzipora, because she was not often with him, but I knew Miriam, his sister, very well. She was very dear to me, and I loved her. When I wasn't with my father Asher's clan, I was with Miriam. When we crossed the Red Sea, I was among the women whom she led in song and dance.[16] As she played her drum, I plucked notes from the harp that I had smuggled out of Egypt. I sang, played, and danced. Our joy and our spirits were luminous.

Q: Were you able to hold on to the joy of this moment throughout your journey?

Serah: I tried. Our lives are only a string of moments, and each one has the potential for joy and greatness. Although we often wish each other long life, as my grandfather Jacob did me, it is these blink-of-an-eye moments that hold the most meaning in the grand scheme of things. The length of a life is only as important as its meaningful moments, strung together to make a story. I kept the joy from that moment with Miriam and the women and used it to build greater meaning to the challenges that we faced in the desert.

Q: In your opinion, what was God's role in these events?

Serah: It is difficult to cling to a God we cannot see and to recognize His power in daily life. It was so difficult in our time, since we were surrounded by those who did not cherish life and freedom or believe in the potential of good in the world, as we did. It was a miracle that we kept our faith. But that is what saved us. Difficult does not mean impossible.

---

[16] Exodus 15:20–21.

Q: Some survivors of the Holocaust of the twentieth century attribute their survival to faith in a benevolent God and a persistent hope in the future.[17]

    Serah: I can understand that. If we are strongly linked to our past, if we have faith in a compassionate God who cares about our future, then the present will always empower us to fulfill our destiny. Our Torah gives us this perspective. It is a powerful tool for survival and for generating wisdom. Our sages believe that wisdom is the ability to see the good in everything.

Q: It is certainly important to stay connected to our past and to our memory as a people. Thank you, Serah bat Asher.

---

[17] Frankl, Viktor E. *Man's Search for Meaning.* New York: Simon & Shuster, 1959.

MIRIAM

MIRIAM, THE DAUGHTER of Amram and Jocheved and the eldest sister of Aaron and Moses, was born in Egypt in approximately 1400 B.C.E. Her life was an expression of her free-flowing and creative spirit, as she sings and dances in the Bible. She also sees an opportunity to save the world in each moment of life.

Miriam was born during the reign of a pharaoh who was determined to reduce the Jewish population of Egypt by forcing them to live under oppressive conditions. Yet she tenaciously held on to the potential for dignity even in that world. She kept alive a greater dream, a vision of what should be.

Miriam became a hero by translating that vision into reality. She convinced her parents to continue to bring children into the world, thus defying Pharaoh's efforts to destroy the Israelites.[1, 2] During her work as a midwife,[3] she saved and nurtured the Jewish baby boys instead of obeying Pharaoh's command to put them to death,[4] and then saved her brother Moses.[5] When the Jews left Egypt, she took along a drum, knowing there would be a time to rejoice. After crossing the Red Sea, she led the Israelite women in song and dance to remind them to be grateful for their freedom rather than fearful of the future. For this, the Bible refers to her as Miriam *ha-neviah* – Miriam the prophetess.[6] As a prophet, she is unique in that she expressed her prophetic vision more in her actions than in her words.

---

[1] BT *Sotah* 12a. *The Chumash,* Stone Edition, 297.
[2] *The Book of Legends,* 60, #13.
[3] BT *Sotah* 11b. *The Chumash,* Stone Edition, 295.
[4] *Book of Legends,* 59–60, #12.
[5] *Exodus* 2:3–10.
[6] Exodus 15:20.

Q: WELCOME, Miriam. Can we call this interview an exclusive?

Miriam: Not exactly. The Bible belongs to everyone. Anyone can bring my story to life by reading it there.

Q: True. Tell us your story.

Miriam: Most people know me as the sister of Moses, who led the Jews out of Egypt. What most people don't know is that I led them out too, but with singing and dancing.

Q: What made you decide to do that?

Miriam: When we left Egypt, most Jews were concerned only with their immediate needs. There was little room for extras, but I took my little drum because I knew that we also had to rejoice. Joy and celebration are also necessary for survival.

Q: Did Moses have a problem with what you did?

Miriam: No. He composed his own song, which later became part of the Jewish daily liturgy. It was my own idea to dance and sing, and that is one of the reasons I'm called a prophet.[7]

Q: What is the link between singing and dancing and prophecy?

Miriam: I had a feeling that a force greater than us was propelling us toward independence and nationhood, even though we still had no land to call our own. We had come to Egypt generations before as a family of seventy and had been enslaved, but nevertheless we grew to number more than a million. After four hundred years, our beliefs and traditions remained intact. It was a miracle. It was all part of a greater plan – that's how I saw it.

Q: Once you finally left Egypt, weren't you afraid of the desert, the unknown? At least in Egypt, you knew what to expect.

Miriam: We thought we did, but things just kept on getting worse. We were restricted and oppressed more and more each day. Pharaoh was killing our newborn sons. We were at great risk of dying as a people.

---

[7] Exodus 15:20.

Q: What was prophetic about dancing?

Miriam: I believed that our God was behind this movement of hundreds of thousands of people on a journey to freedom. That called for singing and dancing.

Q: What was the journey like?

Miriam: Once we had crossed the Sea of Reeds – every single one of us unharmed! – I took my drum from underneath my dress, where I had hidden it. I thought it was better to conceal it rather than have people think that I was out of my mind!

I started to sing, and then grabbed my mother's hand and drew her into a dance. Then I started to play my drum as my mother took another girl's hand, who took another's, and we broke away from the column of people, singing and dancing. Soon we became a great circle of women, including the oldest among us, my mother's cousin Serah bat Asher, and everyone sang and danced while the men and boys watched. Many of them began to clap their hands in rhythm with us as they smiled and laughed.

Q: So you lifted their spirits as well.

Miriam: Oh, yes! When I began singing, our joy and relief burst beyond the words and music into dance. Our bodies became our instruments, expressing everything we felt at that moment.

Q: It sounds wonderful, Miriam. If I had been there, I would have danced too. Only now, I'm thinking about how many times in life we could dance, but we don't.

Moving on: you said that this event was one of the reasons you became known as a prophet. What were the others?

Miriam: As a midwife, I saved Israelite babies. I also convinced my parents, who had decided not to bring any more children into a life of slavery, to get back together and not succumb to hopelessness. My brother Moses was born as a result, and where would we have been without him? But don't forget – dancing was what also defined my prophecy.

You see, although I uttered few prophecies in speech, I expressed Divine insight in my actions. In my case, you see my prophecy rather than hear it. I guarded my baby brother, Moses, because I knew that he was not destined to die. I saved baby boys as a midwife, knowing that they would live to stand at Sinai. I packed a drum, knowing that there would be occasion for us, as a people, to sing and dance.

Q: Can you tell us a bit about these other events?

Miriam: I was born in Egypt. When my grand-uncle Joseph brought our family to settle in the province of Goshen, some of us moved to other cities where they assimilated with the Egyptians. By the time I was born, Joseph was long gone and Egyptian society was faltering under a Pharaoh who was weak and wicked. He used us as scapegoats for his failures. As Egyptian society declined, the Israelite community grew stronger. Pharaoh feared that we would rise up and take over, so he enslaved us.[8]

Q: How were you identifiable as the children of Israel?

Miriam: We Israelites refused to have anything to do with the Egyptian gods. Instead, we worshipped the God of our ancestors Abraham, Isaac and Jacob – a single, invisible God. We gave charity to the poor, Hebrews and Egyptians alike, even when we were slaves. We kept Abraham's tradition of circumcising our male children. We dressed differently from the Egyptians, spoke Hebrew and kept our Hebrew names.[9]

Q: The Bible speaks a great deal about the oppression that the Israelites suffered under Pharaoh. Can you describe the ways in which he oppressed you?

Miriam: Pharaoh tried to break us. He forced shopkeepers to shut down and threw professionals out of their jobs. He forced our men to work at tedious and pointless manual labor. We had to pay outrageous taxes, and we lost our right to be free citizens. Even as we struggled under all of these restrictions, Pharaoh's plans became

---

[8] *The Chumash,* Stone Edition, 293 (commentary on verses 8–14).
[9] *Book of Legends,* 71, #73.

more direct. He ordered all midwives to throw every newborn male into the Nile River.

I was a midwife. My mother, Jocheved, had trained me starting in early childhood, and we often worked together in Pharaoh's household because we were considered the best in our field. When we worked among the Egyptians, we went by our Egyptian names: my mother was called Shifra, and I was called Puah.[10]

Pharaoh's decree against the Hebrew male newborns terrified us. My mother and I risked our lives to defy it. When we delivered a male infant, we would nurse the baby until I could find a family that no one suspected of having a newborn. We would place the mother and baby there, and the children hid for most of their lives until we left Egypt. In my opinion, these families were all heroes. This brings me to my own parents, Amram and Jocheved.

Even though they had wanted more children, they agreed to separate when Pharaoh issued his awful decree. My father feared that my mother wouldn't be able to bear the loss of her baby. As other couples followed their lead, I saw that this could mean the end of our people. This was a complete surrender to Pharaoh, and I wouldn't stand for it.

Q: According to Jewish tradition, you were the one who made them get back together.[11, 12]

Miriam: They loved each other very much and hadn't wanted to separate in the first place. I convinced them to consider the future, to see my vision for our community, and luckily, they agreed.

Q: It seems that adults don't always see as clearly as children do.

Miriam: That's so true – and that can be so frustrating and disappointing for children, since they look to their parents for wisdom. Once my parents remarried, the couples who had followed

---

[10] BT *Sotah* 11b. *The Chumash,* Stone Edition, 295.
[11] BT *Sotah* 12a. *The Chumash,* Stone Edition, 297.
[12] *The Book of Legends,* 60, #13.

them the first time followed them once more, and more Jewish children were born.

Q: You were quite the daughter.

Miriam: Soon after my parents re-united, my brother Aaron was born.

Q: And Moses? When did he come along?

Miriam: My brother Moses was born in the year that you would call 1393 B.C.E. He had a strong voice and deep dark eyes. Since the Egyptians sent patrols throughout our neighborhood all the time, my mother had to nurse him constantly to keep him quiet.

Pharaoh became suspicious when my mother stopped working as a midwife in the palace. One of his officers, whose baby I had saved during a difficult delivery, warned me that they knew about Moses and were about to take him away. In a panic, not knowing what else to do and with no time to make a plan, my mother rushed my baby brother to the river and put him in a basket. She would never have been able to survive the sight of Pharaoh's men taking her child away. And so, together, we set the cradle free on the river, and watched with tears in our eyes as its gentle flow lulled him to sleep.[13]

Q: That must have been so difficult for both of you. What did you do then?

Miriam: I kept my eyes on that basket from the top of a rise and followed it as it floated downstream. I didn't let it out of my sight for a moment.[14] All the time, I prayed hard for my brother's safety. As the river took him near the palace, Moses woke up and started to cry. Pharaoh's daughter, the Princess Bithia, happened to be at the river just then. She heard the cries from the basket as it floated towards her, opened the basket and picked him up. I held my breath.

---

[13] Exodus 2:3.
[14] Exodus 2:4.

Q: What happened next?

Miriam: The princess looked closely at Moses and saw that he was circumcised. She knew that he was a Hebrew baby. It was common knowledge that she was in an unhappy arranged marriage and longed for a child of her own to love – and Moses was an exceptionally beautiful child. On the spot, the Princess Bithia decided to adopt him. Later on we found out that she had given him the name Moses, which comes from the phrase "I drew him from the water."[15]

Q: And then?

Miriam: From my lookout on the other side of the river, I ran home as quickly as I could and told my mother everything. She was so relieved! If Moses was in Pharaoh's palace, then we, as the palace midwives, could arrange for his care, and my mother would be able to nurse him herself. That day, I looked up to the heavens and felt the deepest love for God that can possibly be imagined. I felt His presence so strongly, in a way that I had never felt it before, and I knew that it would not be long until we were finally free.

Q: So you brought your parents back together, leading to your baby brother's birth, and you witnessed God's rescue of that same little brother. Does this mean anyone with a vision can be a prophet?

Miriam: Not necessarily, though it helps to be connected to your spiritual side. In Judaism, it's not only God who chooses who will be a prophet. The person has to accept the job, hear the inner voice and have vision.[16] And even though the Bible calls me a prophet, the rabbis of the Talmud still debated as to whether I really was one, probably because I gave no speeches, preferring to act on my prophecies.[17]

---

[15] Exodus 2:10.

[16] Maimonides. *The Guide of the Perplexed,* vol. 2. Chicago: The University of Chicago Press, 1963. Chapters 31–46, 359–403.

[17] *The Book of Legends,* 60, #16.

Q: How surprising! What did they decide in the end?

Miriam: They never made a final decision. They left the question open.

Q: Do you think you were a prophet or a hero?

Miriam: A hero seizes a moment and does something extraordinary. A prophet's focus is constantly on the extraordinary, on the synchrony between God's hand and life's unfolding. For example, let's say that we do something good and everything falls easily into place. The prophet sees it as God at work with us. This connection is the fiber of a prophet. You asked before whether anyone with vision can be a prophet – well, in this way, we can. We all have that potential.

Q: Would you say that your message to Jewish people today is that they should work on developing their spiritual side?

Miriam: Yes, certainly – but my message is also that children can teach more than any book. If parents are only willing to listen to their children, they will hear clear and powerful messages.

There's something else. Although Passover is the time of year when we concentrate on freedom the most, we can also liberate ourselves from the mundane every day and dance through life with a greater vision for ourselves and our people.

Q: A powerful message indeed. Thank you, Miriam.

TZIPORA

TZIPORA WAS THE WIFE of Moses, the greatest leader and prophet in Jewish history. As with many women throughout Jewish history, Tzipora was a major force in the success of her husband and family. And as with other men in Jewish history, Moses was careful to listen to his wife.

To the extent that she is present in the biblical narrative, Tzipora is a full partner with Moses and a woman of quiet wisdom.

Like Tamar, Tzipora came from a monotheistic, though non-Hebrew, family. She married a Jew and later reminded him of the importance of Jewish custom. Nurtured as a young child by his biological mother, the Jewish woman Jocheved, but educated in the palace of Egypt's Pharaoh, Moses grew up in a mixed cultural background.

In young adulthood, his Jewish memory pulled him back to the God of his ancestors. Later on, Tzipora understood how important it was to him. She encourged his allegiance to his Jewish roots so that he would be able to fulfill his destiny to lead the Jews into freedom and nationhood.

Their story takes place in the Book of Exodus.

Q: WELCOME, Tzipora.

Tzipora: Thank you for inviting me into the present. Are you a Hebrew?

Q: I am, but not all your readers may be. Today, we are called Jews.

Tzipora: I'm flattered and honored that you chose to hear my story. After all, I am not a prominent figure in the Bible.

Q: Speak to us in your words.

Tzipora: I was a farmer's daughter, one of many. My father Reuel, or Yitro as he is known in the Bible, tended herds of sheep and cattle in Midian, an Egyptian province. He was descended from

Abraham and Keturah, the woman he married after Sarah died, whose sons settled in the eastern parts of the continent, now known as Ethiopia.[1] Eventually, my father's family migrated to Egypt and settled in Midian.

My father was also a priest, and the religious leader among our tribes. We were monotheists who lived by the Noahide laws.[2] Although my father was not a Hebrew, he had a Jewish soul and a deep spiritual understanding of Jews.

Q: What was the difference between the Noahide laws and the commandments that the Israelites received?

Tzipora: The difference between ourselves and the Hebrews was that Abraham and his wife Sarah's practice went beyond the Noahide laws and developed a system with six hundred and thirteen commandments based on the Torah.[3] An example of the difference is that although non-Jews and Jews alike are commanded not to steal, Jews were also commanded to give charity to the poor. Jews consider nations who abide by the Noahide laws as righteous nations.

Q: Tzipora, in your time and place a priest had a great deal of power and status. Yet you say that your father was also a farmer and shepherd. How did a priest come to tend sheep in the provinces?

Tzipora: For many years, my father lived at the Egyptian court as one of Pharaoh's advisers. He left the palace and moved to Midian when a new pharaoh, who was narcissistic and abusive, came to power. This pharaoh, who ruled during my youth, suppressed minority groups as well as his own people. He punished

---

[1] Kugel, James L. *The Bible As It Was.* Cambridge: The Belknap Press of Harvard University Press, 1997, 299–300.

[2] *Jewish Literacy,* 509–510.

[3] Torah is defined as "the body of Divine knowledge and law (and which defines) Jewish scriptures and tradition." *The Merriam-Webster Dictionary.* Mass: Merriam-Webster Incorporated, 1997, 762.

them severely if they dared express dissent. He was especially harsh on the Hebrews. He taxed them heavily, driving them into poverty. They were not allowed to own businesses or work in the free professions, and were forced to perform manual labor for the state. They were stripped of their rights as citizens and not allowed to live in dignity.

Q: This sounds very much like what happened in a place called Nazi Germany many centuries after you were born. Like Pharaoh, its rulers tried to kill all Jews who lived there. They also invaded neighboring countries and killed their Jewish populations. The modern State of Israel was established soon after their defeat.

Tzipora: It would seem that each disaster led to a rebirth of the Jewish people as a nation. Strange, isn't it? Catastrophes, rebirths, wisdom from tragedy – it seems that the greatest rewards come from the most difficult of lessons.

Q: Jewish mystical thought also believes that we can reach great heights of knowledge and understanding through suffering. Our hardships can be our greatest teachers, prompting us to choose new paths. According to this teaching, our sufferings are precious.[4] But please go on with your story.

Tzipora: When my father left Pharaoh's palace and settled in Midian, his reputation for justice and wisdom preceded him. He became the leader of the tribes where we settled. His farm grew, he gained many followers, and he prospered.

Q: So your father was doing well, and you grew up. And then you met Moses. How?

Tzipora: One day, I was far from home in the fields with my sisters, trying to draw water for our livestock from an outlying well. Young men from another family approached and began to harass us. They bullied us often, and we knew that we would have to wait hours to water our animals. Suddenly a man appeared, covered in

---

[4] Schneider, Sarah Yehudit. *A Still Small Voice*. 2007. Rosh Hashanah.

dust. Weariness seemed to be carved on his face, but he was handsome. He was tall, with deep-set eyes that seemed to reflect his soul. Even then, I could sense an aura of sadness and thoughtfulness about him.

Q: It sounds like he made quite an impression on you.

Tzipora: Oh, yes! His piercing blue eyes, his thick arched brows that met almost at the centre of his forehead, and his prominent cheekbones were remarkable. It seemed like he had appeared out of nowhere. He confronted the bullies, and it didn't take long for him to send them running. As he bent to roll away the large stone that was covering the well, our eyes met. My heartbeat was never the same again from that moment. That was Moses.

Q: It sounds like that meeting changed your life.

Tzipora: Oh, it did. After he chased away the bullies and helped us water our flocks, I insisted that he come to our home for a meal, and to meet my father. He agreed. My father welcomed Moses warmly after we told him how Moses had helped us. My father and Moses talked privately for hours, sharing their life stories. They had a great deal in common since Moses, like my father, had gotten into trouble by fighting against injustice and had fled from Pharaoh's palace.[5] Moses arrived in Midian hoping to lead a quiet life and rediscover who he really was. His passion for justice and truth made him reject the despotism of Egypt.

And there, just as he arrived in Midian, Moses witnessed another injustice: my sisters and I being bullied at the well. Again, he took action.[6] But this time he found refuge with our family. My father, who was very impressed with Moses, asked him to stay for as long as he wished.

During the first days of Moses's stay with us, my father called us in to hear his story.

---

[5] Exodus 2:11–15.
[6] Ibid.

Q: Imagine hearing Moses tell his own story.

Tzipora: He told us how he had been raised in an Israelite home as a baby, but was later educated at the Egyptian court. He told us of his ambivalence toward the royal court, how he had celebrated their festivals and behaved as a loyal Egyptian subject even as he felt that he was not entirely Egyptian because of his Jewish roots.

Q: How was Moses able to hold onto any connection with his Jewish roots in the palace, amidst all that luxury?

Tzipora: If you have heard my sister-in-law Miriam's story, you might remember that Moses had spent his earliest years in the arms of his mother Jocheved, one of the palace midwives. While Pharaoh's daughter was Moses's legal, adoptive mother, Jocheved nursed him and sang to him in Hebrew, linking his heart to his Hebrew soul. These were the seeds of his truest identity. No luxury that the palace offered could replace the warmth of his Hebrew memories.

When Moses came of age, his yearning for his Hebrew roots drove him to venture outside the palace. As he watched the Hebrews – his own people – hard at their labors, he witnessed an Egyptian beating a Hebrew slave. He intervened and killed the Egyptian. Shortly afterwards, he came upon two Hebrews fighting with each other. When he tried to make peace between them, they taunted him, saying that they knew how he had killed the Egyptian. At that point, Moses knew that he had to run away. It was not only the fact that his act was no longer a secret. It was also his disappointment upon realizing that his own people, whom he had tried to help, could so easily turn on him. He had expected better of the Hebrews.

So he fled to Midian. Just as he arrived, he saw yet another incident of oppression – our incident at the well. He had seen Egyptian oppressing a Jew, a Jew fighting a Jew, and now, non-Jews bullying non-Jews. Immoral behavior was everywhere! But he could

51

not simply let it go on. He could not tolerate injustice.[7] So he intervened again.

Q: All those similar incidents... it sounds like God was trying to give him a message.

Tzipora: I believe that. All these incidents were defining moments in Moses's life – he realized that he was a descendant of Abraham first, with his sense of justice and compassion for his fellow human being, and an Egyptian second – and that only by circumstance.

A short time later, Moses declared his love for me and asked my father for my hand. My father agreed. I was overcome with joy.

Q: You must have been quite a special young lady to have attracted such a man.

Tzipora: I mostly take after my father. I also like to think that I took after my distant ancestor Abraham even a little, that I possessed the sparks of a Jewish soul.

When Moses asked to marry me, nothing cast a shadow on my joy even though I knew that he was a complex man. I became the sister-in-law of the prophet Miriam, whom I had heard so much about. I hoped that when we met, she would approve of me and we would be kindred spirits.

Q: So you and Moses were married....

Tzipora: Our wedding was the most joyous day of my life. The ceremony took place in the Hebrew tradition: under a canopy beneath the stars. Moses's blessings touched my soul so deeply that I had no doubt about adopting his faith. That night he seemed to forget his melancholy, which was his constant companion.

Q: What was it like to be married to Moses?

Tzipora: Moses and I enjoyed only a short time together before he was called to his mission. He shared many details of his life with

---

[7] Telushkin, *Jewish Literacy*, 45.

me, and we became very close. It was clear that he was destined to become a great Jewish leader.

Q: Do you think that a Jewish upbringing in early childhood is a key ingredient in solidifying, or perhaps changing, the direction of a person's life?

Tzipora: It may not necessarily predict where a child will go, but I believe it is an important factor.

Q: Many Jews today choose to abandon Judaism because they had no Jewish experiences, or they had negative ones. Those who have good Jewish memories tend to want to revisit them.

Tzipora: Moses's early quest for truth and justice is what led him back to his birthright. His fate was then to lead others back to it as well.

Q: Did you notice anything change about him as he took on his mission?

Tzipora: After his encounter with God at the burning bush,[8] his face changed. His brow became smooth, the light in his eyes became more intense, and his face shone.

Q: That was his moment of truth – his Sinaitic moment, in a manner of speaking.

Tzipora: It certainly was. And don't think he was eager to do it, either! He refused the job, putting the blame upon his own inadequacy. He had a speech impediment, and above all was extremely humble. But it seems that we can't desist from doing what is right because of our personal issues. God knew whom to choose, and Moses finally agreed. Still, it was his very reluctance to face his obligations as a Hebrew that forced me to do something drastic later on.

Q: What do you mean?

---

[8] Exodus 3 and 4:1–18.

Tzipora: When Moses began his mission to lead the Hebrews out of Egypt, I had just given birth to our second son, Eliezer. Our eldest, Gershom, was already walking. The fatigue of childbirth, adjusting to a second child, and the urgency to leave left me no time to experience joy of our new baby. I didn't even have time to think of parting from my family, which spared me many tears. I thought that we should wait until after Eliezer was circumcised, but there was no discussing this with Moses. He was a changed man, and a charged man whose eyes were fixed far ahead and upward. We left within six days of my giving birth and were fast on our way to Egypt's palace, where Moses would confront Pharaoh and demand that he release the Hebrews — who were, after all, Moses's extended family — and therefore mine.

By now, I was completely committed to his ideals and a full Hebrew partner, for the line I had cast into his spiritual world only drew me closer to Hebrew traditions and rituals. The more I learned of them, the more my perspective on life changed, and the more deeply committed I became. So on the second day of our journey, which was the eighth day after Eliezer's birth, Moses was so engrossed in his mission that he forgot to perform a *brit milah* on his son.

Q: Would you explain the significance of the *brit milah*?

Tzipora: The *brit milah* is a symbol of the covenant that God made with the Hebrews — the Jewish people, as they are known today — to be partners in creation. In one interpretation, it symbolizes the recognition that God created an unfinished world and we are here to help perfect it.[9] Another is that if we live by God's law, God will preserve us — circumcision symbolizes this contract. "It is the oldest ritual in Judaism, going back to Abraham."[10] It is one of the remnants of Jewish life that the

---

[9] *Book of Legends,* 276, #383.
[10] *Jewish Literacy,* 609–610, 53–54.

Hebrews continued to practice even during their exile and slavery in Egypt.

Q: How could such a man as Moses forget this essential ritual?

Tzipora: At the burning bush, when Moses tried to dissuade God from choosing him, God became angry.[11] This seemed to God a rejection of the *brit* – the covenant or partnership – that had been made with Abraham. When it came to performing the *brit milah* while traveling in the desert, Moses was reluctant once again, engulfed in his own fear and anxiety. God was angered again and was about to punish him right then and there – with death! – for neglecting His covenant.

Fearing the worst, I quickly stepped forward and performed the *brit* myself.[12] Moses froze and watched as I performed the mitzvah. Moses re-learned the lesson of the *brit* from *me* – and he also learned that our fears and worries can be self-indulgent and excuses for inaction.

Q: Was it your destiny to refocus Moses, then?

Tzipora: I suppose it was. I, of all people, was the one to remind him of the basics of his faith. Even if that seems unlikely, I was his wife, his partner and the beneficiary of his light and his wisdom. I was also the mother of his children – who else could have understood what must be done? I took the blade, performed the circumcision and threw the evidence in front of him with stern words. From then on, I knew that our married life would be very different.

He realized then that as leader of the Hebrews, his dedication would be solely to his mission. God was his partner and there would be little room for me and our sons in the next stage of his life. He became a person apart. I endured many periods of solitude and loneliness without him, but I also realized that devotion to his

---

[11] Exodus 4:14.
[12] Exodus 4:24–26.

mission was his destiny. I still loved him deeply, and I loved his people.

Q: It sounds as if your performing the circumcision changed everything.

Tzipora: Moses continued on to Egypt to meet his brother Aaron, who would help him negotiate with Pharaoh. Since I could do nothing there, I went back to Midian with our sons.

Q: Did you feel betrayed?

Tzipora: No, never! Staying with him would only have distracted him and complicated the effort. Some leadership comes from being a solid silent partner.

Q: Didn't you ever feel lonely or resentful?

Tzipora: Lonely, yes. But I was proud of Moses and proud to be his wife.

Q: Did you keep living as a Hebrew?

Tzipora: Of course. Not all the Hebrews left in the exodus. I hired some to teach and influence our sons. Several times, we traveled to meet Moses and the Hebrews as they traveled in the desert, and on one of these occasions my father helped Moses to set up a system of higher and lower courts. In this way, the laws could be clarified and applied and the burden of all judgments eased from Moses's shoulders.

After this reunion, I never saw Moses again. When I was lonely, I reached out to help others. Miriam had taught me that this was the best way to overcome fear and sadness. It works. It moved me from selfishness to selflessness, shifted my mood when I helped others, and sent away the clouds.

Q: And what became of your sons, Gershom and Eliezer?

Tzipora: They eventually rejoined their father and when Moses died, they settled in Israel with the Jewish people. My only regret is that our two sons, Gershom and Eliezer, were not with their father at Mount Sinai when God gave us the Ten Commandments.

Q: Interesting. Please tell us about your relationship with Miriam.

Tzipora: The first time I met Miriam, I felt the presence of a great person. I said very little, even though she made me feel comfortable telling me how much she respected me. Can you imagine?

Whenever I was with Miriam, I absorbed what I could of her knowledge and wisdom, which came from her broad vision of the world. We loved each other dearly, and I almost cried more each time I said goodbye to her than when I did when I parted from Moses. Although I will never know for sure, I imagine that it was because we shared a relationship with such a great man and bore its joys and difficulties together. Miriam had an aura around her, as did Moses. She brought joy and optimism wherever she went, while Moses had to carry a heavy load.

Q: Do you think the strong physical attraction that you and Moses shared belied your deep spiritual commitment to each other? Do you think that a good leader needs a strong partner?

Tzipora: Miriam and I were always behind him. We shared great pride and joy in helping a leader who went beyond human boundaries.

Women seem to have a strong natural ability to enable others. But any true partner can move the other beyond his or her limits and find a Moses inside them.

Q: Yes, indeed. Thank you, Tzipora.

MAHLAH, NOA, HOGLAH, MILCAH, AND TIRZAH

THE DAUGHTERS OF ZELOPHEHAD

THE MERE FACT that the Bible names the daughters of Zelophehad – Mahlah, Noa, Hoglah, Milcah, and Tirzah – gives each of them importance in Jewish history. They claimed their legal right to inherit land in Canaan when the custom was that only sons or male descendents could inherit. Their knowledge and advocacy skills changed the Hebrew inheritance laws and the manner in which they are applied to this day. Since Zelophehad, their father, was a descendant of Menasheh, Joseph's elder son, the daughters could trace their lineage back. Mahlah, Noa, Hoglah, Milcah, and Tirzah knew their history.

The Bible tells their story at the last stop in the desert, before the Jews were about to enter Canaan after having spent forty years in the wilderness.[1] On this journey, they carried the bones of their ancestor Joseph, fulfilling the promise that the Hebrews of that time had made to him.

At this last stop in the desert, before entering Canaan, a census was taken in order to determine all those among whom the land would be divided.[2] To their dismay, the daughters of Zelophehad discovered that their names were not on the list.

Upset by this omission, they agreed that they should not be disqualified from inheriting a rightful share of the Promised Land, especially given their lineage, just because their parents had had no son. They used knowledge, good timing, and preparedness to

---

[1] Numbers 27:1–9.
[2] Numbers 26:53.

present their argument to Moses, pleading for the dignity of their father's memory. They are role models of advocacy for what is just and right.

Q: WE ARE HONORED to have Tirzah, a representative of the five daughters of Zelophehad, to speak with us now. Today she and her sisters would constitute a law firm. Yet almost thirty-three hundred years ago, they were a group of young women who were as astute and knowledgeable as any young lawyer is today. Tirzah tells their story.
Tirzah: Thank you.

Q: Would you tell us a little about yourself and your family?
Tirzah: We were descended from the tribe of Menasheh, Joseph's elder son. Like our ancestor Joseph, we wanted very much to live in the land that God had promised to the Hebrews. We were also committed to fulfilling the vow that our ancestors had made to Joseph as he was dying: to take his bones out of Egypt and bury them in Canaan when they returned.

Q: Today there are still many Jews who live outside of Israel but wish to buried there. How is it that you loved Israel so much if you had never been there?
Tirzah: We knew our history. We cherished it as much as we cherished our dream to settle in Canaan. For forty years my family carried our ancestor Joseph's bones, and we knew that each day brought us closer to the longed-for day when we could bring our direct ancestor, from five generations back, to his final resting place. As we carried his casket, slowly and steadily, Moses would cast his eyes protectively on it like a safety net, much the same as Miriam had watched him float down the Nile a generation before.

Then, one terrible day during the journey, our dear father, Zelophehad, died of old age. An honorable man, he had never participated in any of the revolts or complaints of the people against Moses. We buried him in the wilderness and mourned for him.

When the census was taken in order to divide the land, we were shocked to discover that we were not on the list. We could not understand the reason. Why should our family remain landless just because our father had no son?

Q: You knew the laws of the time. Why would you have expected otherwise? Women did not inherit property.

Tirzah: Exactly. The law was as you say, but that doesn't mean that it was just. We are not named because we had no male survivors in our family. The injustice of this situation upset us, and my sisters and I agreed that it was not right. Five highly individual sisters, as we were, don't agree about many things, but we were unanimous in our feeling that we were being discriminated against because we were women. We asked ourselves and each other: Why should we be penalized, why should we not be given a portion of our own, merely because we are females? We could not let this injustice pass.[3] The thought that we did not deserve an inheritance solely because we were women upset us terribly. Why should our line, which reached back to Joseph, be cut off in such a way? As we saw it, this was anathema to our people.[4]

Q: Only a few minutes ago, you told us how proud you all were that your father had never rebelled or challenged Moses. How could you think of doing so yourselves? After all, you were young and inexperienced, and you saw how the other people who had challenged Moses – who were far older than you – had paid dearly. Weren't you afraid?

Tirzah: My sisters and I thought long and hard about what we should do and what others had done. We decided to present a case to Moses in a timely and educated manner. The foundation of our case would rest on the merits of our lineage and the injustice of gender discrimination, not on anger or rebellious motives. Surely

---

[3] Schneider, Susan. "The Daughters of Zelophehad." In *Torah of the Mothers,* edited by Ora Wiskind Elper and Susan Handelman, 156.

[4] *Reading the Women of the Bible,* 108.

the God of all humankind did not mean to end a branch of Joseph's lineage, or suppress a family's pure love of Israel.

Q: And Moses was receptive to hearing your case. It seems that he was used to his people bringing all sorts of issues to him.

Tirzah: You may recall that Yitro, Moses's father-in-law, helped him set up a system of courts so that lesser cases could be brought before elders and the important ones brought before Moses. It was an enhanced application of the Noahide laws that are fundamental to a civilized society and that apply to all nations.[5] Our case went before Moses quickly since it involved a ruling that went beyond personal concerns. It would affect our entire community, the entire collective of Israel, since we were arguing laws of inheritance that would affect future generations.

Q: What were your arguments?

Tirzah: We had five arguments, and here they are:

1. Zelophehad, our father, was a good man. He had never complained about Moses or been rebellious, and therefore deserved a share and stake in the land of Canaan.
2. Our father had no son.
3. We daughters were as much direct descendants as sons would have been, and through our children, we would perpetuate the lineage of Joseph.
4. We, too, had come out of Egypt and accepted the Ten Commandments at Mount Sinai in good faith. We obeyed the laws faithfully, to the best of our ability.
5. Our branch of Joseph's family tree deserved the same honor and portion of Israel as all the other branches that stemmed from the patriarch Jacob. We deserved not to be overlooked, disqualified or robbed of our inheritance merely because we were women.

We ended our plea by describing how much we yearned for the Promised Land as we stood on its threshold. We declared our

---

[5] *Jewish Literacy,* 509–510.

willingness to live there by the laws that God had given us at Mount Sinai and in the desert. We spoke of our gratitude for God's graciousness in bringing us to this point. What better citizens could the new nation want than we? Our words in the Torah are: "Why should the name of our father be omitted (cut off) from among his family because he had no son? Give us a possession among our father's brothers."[6]

Q: How did Moses respond?

Tirzah: He was speechless. Imagine! Moses, the greatest prophet, the liberator and leader of our people, the recipient of the Ten Commandments at Sinai, the only prophet ever to have spoken directly with God, had no answer! And so, in keeping with his humility and ability to turn to a higher authority, he brought our claim before God.[7]

Q: Impressive. He is a model of the perfect leader.

Tirzah: What is really impressive is God's answer to Moses. He said, "The daughters of Zelophehad have spoken properly,"[8] which meant that He approved of what we had said. And so, in a precedent-setting ruling, all future laws of inheritance were changed to allow a woman to inherit if there were no male descendants. I understand that these laws are still referred to in your present time and used to settle inheritance disputes.[9]

Q: They are indeed. By presenting your case in such a wise way that you were able to win it, you helped many women whom you would never meet. We owe you a great debt of gratitude.

What happened next?

Tirzah: When we entered Canaan, we received our rightful share of land and settled there, living in peace and security.

---

6 Numbers 27:4.

7 Numbers 27:5.

8 Numbers 27:7.

9 Deen, Elizabeth. *All the Women of the Bible.* New Jersey: Castle Books, 1955, 62–64.

Q: As you certainly deserved. What lessons can you share with us from your experience?

Tirzah: Learning yields power, and good timing is extremely important! If one is fortunate enough to live in a democracy, one must be ready, armed with facts and wise enough to know when the time is right to present one's case. The right argument, the ability to make that argument to the right person, and good timing are all very important for a successful outcome.[10, 11]

Q: We have an expression in our day: "Timing is everything."

Tirzah: How true! Not only that, though: what we say, to whom we say it, and the way in which we say it are all very important. My sisters and I learned so much from the experience. Moses also gave us a gift: a lesson in humility. Moses was our community's leader and its highest judge, and yet he was not ashamed to admit that he didn't have the answer. He didn't hesitate to consult a higher authority. We felt he gave us another lesson, too – that in life, our partner in solving many of our problems may be the very One who created us.

Q: Are you suggesting that God can give us answers?

Tirzah: I believe that we can listen for God to speak to us when we pause, sit quietly, and allow ourselves to feel the harmony in what seems right. The opposite is also true, but either way, we can be receptive to Divine messages if we make space for them. Truth is not loud or aggressive. It is soft, sure and subtle – that proverbial "still small voice" within all of us. My sisters and I felt it, and we created the opportunity to act upon it.

Q: Tirzah, we are almost out of time. But before we close, you and your sisters might enjoy knowing that the Talmud commends you all for your "intuitive sense of timing, as well as your learnedness in

---

10 Magriso, R.Y. *Yalkut Me'Am Loez, The Torah Anthology*. New York/Jerusalem: Magnum Publishers, 256.

11 BT *Bava Batra* 119b; *Deuteronomy Rabbah,* 21:11.

the way you formulated your arguments before Moses, using principles and precedents."[12]

Tirzah: It is good to know that our sages appreciate what we did. Thank you for telling us!

Q: Not only that. Modern women scholars have taken your story as a paradigm of the "flexibility (of Jewish law) to expand and embrace women, giving us increasingly more rights and a fairer share of our common legacy."[13] Some admire your "respectful dialogue, honoring the system, honoring truth and finding a way to transform personal wisdom into Oral Torah. There is no other option."[14] In short, your story has been well recognized by modern scholars. *Brava* to all of you!

Tirzah: On behalf of my sisters, I thank you.

---

[12] BT *Bava Batra* 19b.

[13] Frankel, Ellen. *The Five Books of Miriam.* San Francisco: Harper San Francisco, 1996, 236.

[14] "The Daughters of Zelophehad." In *Torah of the Mothers,* 161.

HANNAH

HANNAH, THE WIFE of Elkanah and the mother of the prophet Samuel, lived in Israel in approximately 1000 B.C.E. Jewish tradition considers her to be one of seven principal women prophets.[1] Her story takes place in Shiloh, which was the "central point for all Israel... and in the heart of the hill-country which Joshua first subdued"[2] after the Exodus. Hannah is a hero because she is the first woman we know of who dared to argue with God about her unhappy life situation. Her extraordinary confrontation with God provides us with a model for a personal and meaningful relationship with Him. Hannah teaches us not only how to pray, but also the meaning of prayer.

The biblical Patriarch Abraham, who lived long before Hannah, had argued with God for the sake of the inhabitants of Sodom and Gomorrah, pleading that He not destroy righteous people together with wicked ones.[3] But Abraham's interaction was as a leader and representative of the community. Hannah takes our relationship with God one step further. Her story illustrates that aside from communal prayer, each one of us can experience God personally. Our personal prayers may even "project to God how we should be."[4]

Hannah makes us ask ourselves what we pray for and why. Is what we pray for always the best thing for us? She reveals to us that what we pray for is a reflection of what is in our hearts and who we strive to be – that "prayer is the worship of the heart."[5] Moreover,

---

[1] *Megillah* 14a–b.
[2] I Samuel 4:11.
[3] Genesis 18:23–33.
[4] Hartman, David. Global Beit Midrash of the Shalom Hartman Institute. Session 1 (2007).
[5] Steinsaltz, Adin. *The Thirteen-Petalled Rose*. New York: Basic Books, 2006, 129–130.

"when we point to God and blame God for evil, maybe God is pointing at us."[6]

Hannah also makes us think about why prayer is apparently not always answered, and whether the answer *No* can be as meaningful as *Yes*. "At a time when women's voices weren't heard in the sanctuaries and men were the priests, Hannah speaks straight to the Eternal."[7]

Hannah also defines the quality of grace, the Hebrew meaning of her name. She is extraordinary in the dignity she brings to a situation that was full of pain, humiliation, and anguish. Now we hear her story.

Q: THANK YOU for agreeing to be interviewed, Hannah. Would you tell us a little about yourself?

Hannah: I lived in Israel in 1050 B.C.E. My husband was Elkanah, a prophet, a Levite and a descendant of the biblical Korah.[8] I was actually Elkanah's first wife. Peninna, my co-wife, was his second.

Q: Scholars write about how Elkanah loved you more than he did Peninna. How did the household work with two wives, one of whom was more beloved than the other?

Hannah: The Bible describes our relationship as follows: "But to Hannah he gave a double portion, for he loved Hannah...."[9] But much of Elkanah's love for me was out of pity. I had no children of my own, and was terribly unhappy because I wanted them so much. Peninna had borne Elkanah ten children, while I had none!

---

[6] Hartman, David. Global Beit Midrash.

[7] Pravder Mirkin, Marsha. "She Is a Tree of Life: What We Learn from Our Biblical Foremothers. Hannah – Voice, Freedom and Grace." From the Shalom Hartman Tichon Seminar, 2008, compiled by David Dishon and Noam Zion, 50.

[8] Numbers 16.

[9] I Samuel 1:5.

Q: I should think that Elkanah's preference for you, together with Peninna's fruitfulness, would have caused a lot of tension in the household. How did you and Peninna get along?

Hannah: Unfortunately, there was a great deal of friction between us. Peninna was cruel and taunted me. Even the Bible mentions – twice – how she did her best to annoy me.[10]

Q: The Bible also describes how you took her behavior in silence. You wept and didn't eat, but you never responded to her. Fittingly, your name Hannah is derived from the Hebrew word *hen*, meaning grace. Is this the meaning of your silence?

Hannah: I never stooped to Peninna's level. Perhaps this is grace. Or perhaps it was my obsession over the fact that I had no children. Truth to tell, I was more angry with God than I was with Peninna. And so I bore the pain in silence.

Q: Did Elkanah ever try to alleviate the tension between you and Peninna?

Hannah: In our day, the head of the household paid little attention to what happened in the home. It was up to the women to make sure that the home environment was peaceful so that the children would thrive.

Q: Your response is quite different from that of our foremother, Sarah, who expelled her rival, Hagar, from her home.

Hannah: Everyone is different. I focused my energies inward in order to build up the courage to confront God, the only One who could satisfy my need for a child.

Q: Before we discuss your confrontation with God, tell us how you felt when, at one point, your husband Elkanah tried to console you by saying, "Am I not better to you than ten children?"[11] The Bible does not record your answer. Did you give him one?

---

[10] I Samuel 1:6–7.
[11] I Samuel 1:8.

67

Hannah: No, I didn't say anything. I suppose that I was living up to my name by bringing dignity to the situation. My silence never meant I agreed with Peninna or Elkanah. I believed in the power of words. Words are powerful and only useful when they are used wisely. I knew that Elkanah was trying to comfort me, but I also knew that he could never understand that my anguish had nothing to do with our love for each other. Perhaps no man can truly understand a woman's yearning for children.

Q: But you didn't hesitate to speak in Shiloh, when the High Priest, Eli, misunderstood you.

Hannah: Yes, in Shiloh I spoke. Our family made an annual pilgrimage to Shiloh, in central Israel, in order to visit the sanctuary that Joshua had built to hold the Tablets given at Mount Sinai. Every year we would take a different route so that others could join us along the way. Elkanah was a devout man and a leader by example – very graceful in his own way.

In Shiloh, we would make offerings, and following the rituals, all the pilgrims would share meals together before returning home. It was there that Elkanah gave me double portions, but I wouldn't eat. He implored me to eat and drink, if only in reverence to the place and the occasion.

Peninna taunted me there, too. Unlike at home, in Shiloh I always found a place where I could be by myself and cry. All the prayer and celebration was focused on thanksgiving, but I felt that I had little to be thankful for. I had been waiting and praying for a child for almost twenty years.

In the twentieth year of my marriage, I agreed to eat with other pilgrims. I was teetering toward accepting my situation, and as I sat with everyone, I experienced a sudden moment of inspiration. In that year, after the festive dinner, I returned to the sanctuary, where the rituals and communal prayers took place. Eli, the High Priest and the leader of the community, sat in his place by the door, guarding the sanctuary as he always did. He was tired but satisfied that he had seen another successful pilgrimage. He smiled when I approached, but ignored me as I stood and began to pray with every fiber of my heart and soul. My lips moved, but only I heard the words. I cried and vowed to God that if I were to have a son, he would be a lifelong Nazirite, dedicated to the service of God.

Q: Did you really think you could determine the life of your future child?

Hannah: No. Nor does any parent have the right to do so under normal circumstances. But if this child was born in direct response to my prayer to God, then he would be quite a special child, and he would belong to God.[12]

Q: While Jewish figures before and after you thanked and praised God, you are known for challenging and negotiating with God. Your struggle was a bold demand for justice. What gave you the courage to be so forceful with Divine authority?

Hannah: I don't think that God is some creature who coldly decides what will or will not be. That idea may belong to other faiths, but not to mine. Our God, Who brought us to freedom and nationhood, is both a communal and a personal God, Who is involved with each person to the extent that they choose. So if I feel a personal relationship with God, then we can talk.

Q: In your prayer, you are the first to address God as Lord of Hosts (*Adonai Tzevaot*). What does that phrase mean to you?

Hannah: Hosts are souls. God is the only One who could create one to be my child. And so I began my prayer that way.

Q: In the Talmud, Rabbi Eliezer says that you were questioning and even challenging God. His interpretation of your prayer is: "Out of all the hosts of hosts that You created in Your world, is it so difficult for You to give me one son?" – Rabbi Eliezer comments that on seeing so many Jews gathered in Shiloh on pilgrimage, you would say to God: "Master of the Universe, You have all these

---

[12] Abarbanel's commentary on I Samuel 1:11. In *The Prophets, Samuel I*. ArtScroll Series, The Rubin Edition, edited by Rabbi Nosson Scherman and Rabbi Meir Zlotowitz. New York: Mesorah Publications, 2006, 5.

hosts, but among them not even one is mine."[13] Would you say that Rabbi Eliezer understood you?

Hannah: Yes. He captures not only my prayers, but also my anger.

Q: In a story from slightly before my time known as *Tevye the Dairyman,* a father, Tevye, engages with God in a similar way. Tevye argues, laughs, bargains, and struggles with God. "Am I really the world's greatest sinner that I deserved to be its most punished Jew? God in heaven, who am I that You don't forget me even for a second, that You can't invent a new calamity, a new catastrophe, a new disaster, without first trying it out on me?"[14]

Hannah: If one believes in God and reaches a point of desperation, it makes sense to confront God.

The priest Eli reprimanded me because he thought I was drunk. While people sometimes prayed in silence, I was shaking and my lips were moving. "How long are you going to be drunk?" he asked me. "Go sober up!" When I explained that I was praying so fervently out of desperation, he apologized and gave me a blessing that my prayer would be fulfilled.

Q: How did you feel after your prayer?

Hannah: First Samuel 1:18 describes it best: "Then the woman went on her way and she ate, the look on her face was no longer the same." I felt peace in my heart for the first time in many years. It was no longer about my prayer being answered as much as it was about knowing that I could trust God enough to express my innermost fears and needs in prayer. My peace came not from turning away, but by being with God, the same way we may feel when we have spoken truthfully with one we love. I vowed to

---

[13] BT *Berakhot* 31b. "The Talmud." In The Shalom Hartman Tichon Seminar, 2008, compiled by David Dishon and Noam Zion, 13.
[14] Aleichem, Sholem. *Tevye the Dairyman and the Railroad Stories.* New York: Schocken Books, 1996.

honor that personal relationship by accepting whatever the outcome might be.

Q: If your prayer had not been answered, how would you have honored that relationship?

Hannah: By accepting what God had decreed for me. I would have had to accept that what I thought was right for me evidently was not. I would have continued my search for my purpose in this world.

Q: The Talmud contains a lengthy discussion that cites you as the paradigm for prayer, especially when the Second Temple was destroyed, since with the priesthood gone, the Jew's relationship with God had to be more personal. The Talmud also uses you as a model of many ethical norms in life.

Hannah: How interesting! Can you give me some examples?

Q: From the words that describe how you prayed – *al libah* ("upon her heart" or "from her heart") – we learn about the need to have focus and intention in prayer.

From the phrase "Only her lips moved, but her voice was not heard" we learn that we must speak each word clearly in prayer, but may not raise our voices. Prayer must be audible only to the one who is praying. This protects the dignity of those who may be confessing their sins.

From Eli's apology to you: "Go in peace. May the God of Israel grant the request you have made of Him" – we learn that he who wrongfully suspects his fellow man must not only conciliate with him, but also bestow a blessing on him.

From your defense of the fervor of your prayer to Eli – "No, my lord, I am a woman of aggrieved spirit. I have drunk neither wine nor strong drink, and I have poured out my soul before God" – we learn that those who are wrongly suspected must defend themselves and make their innocence known.[15]

---

[15] BT *Berakhot* 31a–b. Shalom Hartman Tichon Seminar, 2008, 11.

Hannah: All that just from my prayer? Who would ever have believed it? Thank you for telling me!

Q: The Bible tells us that when God granted you a son, you kept your vow to give him to Eli to be raised as a Nazarite. Did this defeat the purpose of having a child, since you knew that you would not keep him?

Hannah: The name that I chose for my son, Samuel, has two meanings: *I requested him from God* and *his name is God*. It wrenched my heart to turn him over to Eli when he was still so very young, but I kept the vow I had made to God. I had the pleasure of watching him grow into a fine leader who became "a master of prophets"[16] compared even to Moses and Aaron,[17] and I was so proud to see that when he eventually became a judge, he still went out of his way to help people. It was my son Samuel who was chosen to anoint the first kings of Israel, Saul and David.

Q: Some claim that you made your vow out of desperation, or out of hope that other children would follow, and that "this arrangement, despite common talk about faith and grace, is a sad one."[18]

Hannah: Sad? I was proud! My son merited to have two books of the Bible named after him! And you must not think that I gave him up completely. Even though Samuel grew up at Shiloh rather than at home with me, he did not lack a mother's love. I visited him often and made his clothes for him.

Q: And you had more children after him. Not everyone's prayer is answered as yours was.

Hannah: In personal prayer, we search our souls and ask for what we *think* we need. But sometimes we are unable to see that

---

[16] *Midrash Tehillim.*

[17] Steinsaltz, Adin. *Biblical Images.* New York: Basic Books, 1984, 134.

[18] Fewell, Dana, and David Gunn. "Possessed and Disposed: Hannah." In *Gender, Power, and Promise.* Shalom Hartman Tichon Seminar, 2008, 28.

what we ask for may not be the best for ourselves. In such cases, even unanswered prayers can be a blessing.

After I had borne five more children, I wrote my song, in which I expressed my gratitude to God and my philosophy of life. Today, the song is known as "The Prayer of Hannah" and is recited in Oriental Jewish communities before the morning prayer.

Q: Tell us about your song.

Hannah: I first sang it under prophetic influence, and saw many things that would befall the Jewish people throughout history. Here are some of them:

"The bow of the mighty is broken, while the foundering are girded with strength"[19] – As I sang this sentence, I saw that there would be times in Jewish history when the Jews would prevail over stronger and more numerous enemies.

"The barren woman bears seven, while the one with many children becomes bereft"[20] – Here I saw how Rome, which destroyed the Second Temple and exiled the Israelites, would one day be bereft of its inhabitants,[21] while the children of Jerusalem would return to fill the city.

I also wrote that life is tenuous and the key to life is in God's hands.[22] On the other hand, prayer and righteous acts can bring about change. I expressed it as, "He guards the steps of His devout ones, but the wicked are stilled in darkness; for not through strength does man prevail."[23]

Q: Were you warning us that we often feel too safe in our lives, or were you reminding us to be righteous?

Hannah: Both.

---

[19] I Samuel 2:4.

[20] I Samuel 2:5.

[21] I Samuel 2. *Targum.* The Rubin Edition, 13.

[22] I Samuel 2. *Radak.* The Rubin Edition, 15.

[23] I Samuel 2:9.

Q: Your song ends as if you had fully developed not only personally, but as a prophet with a "communal voice."[24]

Hannah: I prayed not only for Samuel but for all of Israel to succeed through him. I wrote, "May He [that is, God] give power to His king and raise the pride of His anointed one."[25] Here I was seeing the future king, David, whom Samuel would choose and from whom the Messiah would descend.[26] I was singing for all generations of Jews.

Q: We read your story on Rosh Hashanah when the community gathers together to pray. Many people find communal prayer difficult – rote and meaningless. What would you say to those who feel this way?

Hannah: While communal prayer is important, I suggest that part of any prayer should be personal and come from the depth of one's own heart. For example, one may focus on a small part of the liturgy and use it to form one's own prayer to God. It takes a very personal moment to search for what is truly important in one's life. "The hardest and single most important work of each life is to sort through one's desires, and identify those that are authentically true to the depths of one's soul…. At a certain point in the struggle… personal desire melds with Divine Will and we enter through the door of pure prayer [that I seemed to have] opened for all generations…. Our own prayer gets pressed from the depths of our soul."[27]

Q: In the Talmud, Rabbi Eliezer says that we learn how to pray from you and that you teach us to get in touch with our needs. He

---

[24] Praver Mirkin, Marsha. "She is a Tree of Life: What We Learn from our Biblical Foremothers. Hannah – Voice, Freedom, and Grace." In *Shalom Hartman Tichon Seminar*, 2008, compiled by David Dishon and Noam Zion, 50, n. 6.

[25] I Samuel 2:10.

[26] *Yalkut Shimoni.* I Samuel 2. Rubin Edition, 15.

[27] Schneider, Sarah Yehudit. "Time Trekking: Lesson 15." In *A Still Small Voice*, Jerusalem, 1988.

feels that prayer should be *that* personal. How do you resolve the need for personal prayer with the community's need to pray together?

Hannah: Both are necessary. We need community prayer to remind us of the norms of reverence and piety, and it is also important to pray for others. The Israelite community has prayed together since the beginning of our history, when we all contributed to building the Tabernacle in the desert to house the Tablets that bore the Ten Commandments, and since Joshua set up a Tent of Meeting in Gilgal when we arrived in Israel, and then in Shiloh. This brought people together to rally towards the values that sustained us.

Q: In Jewish tradition, ten seems to be the minimum number that defines a community. Rabbi Yitzhak of the Talmud says, "Wherever ten persons pray, the *Shechinah*, the Divine Presence, dwells among them."[28]

Hannah: Yet personal and communal prayers are not mutually exclusive. One can have personal prayer even during communal prayer. Even the formal liturgy sets aside a place for it.

Q: Some rabbis in the Talmud feel that your prayer is too anguished and that prayer should combine reverence with a sense of joy in life.[29] What do you think of their comments?

Hannah: As important as reverence and joy are, when we pray we must remain true to our innermost selves. Since prayer is communication with God, we must cultivate a relationship with God in which we can share all our feelings openly and honestly, whatever they may be.

Q: Thank you, Hannah.

---

[28] *Sanhedrin* 39a.
[29] *Berakhot* 30b–31a. Shalom Hartman Tichon Seminar, 2008, 9.

DEBORAH

DEBORAH'S STORY appears in chapters four and five of the Book of Judges, which recounts the religious and historical development of Israel after the Exodus from Egypt when the Jews conquered Canaan and settled there. Deborah is not only one of Judaism's seven women prophets,[1] but in her story, she is also described as a wife, a judge, and a warrior. Rabbinic lore adds that she had a business where she made wicks for the candles that burned in the Tabernacle which housed the Tablets upon which the Ten Commandments were written.[2] In her story, Deborah refers to herself simply as "a mother in Israel."[3] Although she seems humble, she is not, as we will see in the song she wrote. She is a hero for recognizing and embracing her talents and directing them towards the good of the community in which she lived. She is a "whole person [well-rounded], not eccentric, [but] an individual who tastes perfection in the overall experience of life."[4]

The period in which Deborah lived is known in Jewish history as the period of the Early Prophets, which spans the entry of the Jews into Canaan until the destruction of the First Temple in Jerusalem, in 586 B.C.E.

What was a prophet? The philosopher Maimonides, who wrote extensively about prophecy in his work, *The Guide of the Perplexed*,[5] believed that anyone born with certain qualities, including humility and knowledge, has the potential to be a prophet. He also believed

---

[1] *Megillah* 14a–b.
[2] Ginzberg, Louis. *The Legends of the Jews.* Volume IV. Translated by Henrietta Szold. Philadelphia: JPS, 1913.
[3] Judges 5:7.
[4] Steinzaltz, Adin. *Biblical Images.* New York: Basic Books, 1984.
[5] Maimonides, Moses. *The Guide of the Perplexed.* Volume II. Chicago: The University of Chicago Press, 1963.

that there are various levels of prophecy. He wrote that prophecy can come to one whose qualities of mind and spirit, religious imagination and special virtues – including inner joy – bring a flash of Divine insight to the world. From this perspective, Jewish prophets differ from those of other religions because rather than God selecting the prophet, the Jewish prophet chooses God. Prophets elevate themselves through learning and knowledge and then share their insights with the world.

Maimonides states that all Jews have the potential to achieve this because, as he believes, part of every Jew's soul was present at Mount Sinai and heard the voice of God utter the first two of the Ten Commandments: *I am the Lord thy God, who brought you out of the land of Egypt, out of the house of bondage* and *You shall have no other gods before Me.* This belief gives rise to his assertion that all Jews are potentially able to connect to their Divine nature and develop their spirituality towards a level of prophecy.

Jewish prophets were charismatic, insightful and knowledgeable figures. They were recognized and respected by everyone including by the elders of the community. Prophets did not predict the future. Instead, they gave warning of it. Since their main interest was in justice, morality and the future of the community they attempted to guide the people to moral and spiritual paths in a world of threatening influences.

Modern Jewish philosophers like Jill Hammer remain fascinated with the notion of prophecy. In *Sisters at Sinai,* she writes that prophecy is "a form of wisdom" – a state of being highly attuned to one's spiritual nature in partnership with a Divine Creator.[6] Conversely, the songwriter Paul Simon wrote, "The words of the prophets are written on the subway walls and in tenement halls."[7]

Leaders in Deborah's time referred to her as a prophet because of her knowledge and application of the Ten Commandments in a

---

[6] Hammer, Jill. *Sisters at Sinai.* Philadelphia: JPS, 2004.
[7] Simon, Paul. "The Sounds of Silence." *The Sounds of Silence.* Columbia Records: 1964.

compassionate and just manner, and her strength to fight for their guiding principles. Here is her story.

Q: DEBORAH, in addition to being a prophet, you were a judge, a military leader, an artisan, and a wife and mother. Each of these roles comes with great responsibility and could be a full-time job in itself. How did you balance them? What was a typical day like for you?

Deborah: The backdrop to all my responsibilities was my role as prophet, always being aware of God's presence in the everyday physical world and interpreting life from this perspective. The prophet sees that the spiritual side of humanity needs to find expression through goodness – good deeds that unify humankind in peace. We are always thinking how we, as people, can share in that task for *good*. This idea, which pervades all our words and actions, is a prophet's full time pre-occupation – how to confront every misdeed, enemy, or unkindness and bring truth and justice to the situation. This attitude is particularly important in times of prosperity. But I lived in an unstable time during Jewish history.

Q: Is this how you were drawn into a military role?

Deborah: Yes, it was, but this was nothing new. Prophets were often strategists who decided when to go into battle. Israel was constantly threatened by neighboring countries that wanted to destroy us. These threats weakened the moral fiber of our people, and I understood that we needed both prayer and action to sustain us.

Q: Shimon Peres, a famous Israeli politician of the twentieth and twenty-first centuries, says the same thing about Israel today: that it lives in a "bad neighborhood," surrounded by enemies who wish to destroy it.

Deborah: The more things change….

Q: Let's backtrack a bit. Describe a typical day in your life.

Deborah: I made light – literally. Since the wicks that I made were thicker than usual, they burned longer and more brightly in the Tabernacle, where we worshipped and where my husband worked. His job was to tend the altar lamps, including the permanent light that was kept burning before the ark where the Tablets from Mount Sinai were stored. My wick-making was a small cottage industry, and as I sat at my work, twisting and braiding, people would come to sit with me, discussing life and the issues of our community. In time, they began to ask me for guidance and for messages of hope and inspiration.

Q: I have read that the sages like to interpret your work of making broader wicks as a way of making sure that the people of your day studied the Torah for longer periods of time, keeping it alive in order to illuminate their lives. They applied all these metaphors to your cottage industry. What do you think of their interpretation?[8]

Deborah: I like it very much. I hope it is a way of keeping my own story alive and meaningful. The stories of Torah are meant to be re-interpreted in ways that inspire each individual generation, which is what makes the Torah such a living document.

Q: From whom did *you* learn?

Deborah: I had a strong belief in God from my earliest childhood. I was naturally inclined to understand that every spiritual interpretation of the world made perfect sense. I became a prophet through my optimism. I reached out to others and encouraged them not to give in to fear and material distractions.

The elders chose me as a prophet and judge because I used Torah principles to advise people and mediate disputes. People came to me to learn and to solve the problems that they were having with their family, their neighbors and their faith. God's words provided comfort and, in many cases, solutions. This is how I became a judge.

---

[8] From a lecture by Barbara Sutnick on Deborah during which she cited the midrashic material in Ginzberg's *The Legends of the Jews,* vol. 4.

Q: It seems as though Torah was your law degree. Was there a higher court than yours?

Deborah: Yes. The community had a higher court made up of elders replacing the ones whom Moses chose to help him interpret the Ten Commandments when the Israelites were in the desert. These elders delegated responsibilities for community affairs to others, such as myself.

Q: So people would come to your home?

Deborah: I held court under a palm tree so that I could talk with men without arousing suspicion and gossip.[9] My wick-making also moved to the outdoors, but when my reputation for advice and mediations grew, my little industry suffered.

Q: Multi-tasking is never easy.

Do you think you were a good judge? You were obviously a spiritual person, learned, and a good businesswoman. But weren't you a bit too removed from the details of people's everyday lives to understand their problems?

Deborah: I think that my knowledge of the Torah made me a good judge. It is said, "God looked into the Torah and created the world."[10] Torah is a blueprint of life. It gives its lessons in the form of metaphor and its narratives teach us how to solve problems. Don't be misled by misconceptions of what Torah and spirituality are all about.

Q: Religion's reputation has suffered quite a bit of damage throughout history.

Deborah: Only because people have misused and abused it for personal gain. When religion is used properly, it can be a powerful tool to repair the world.

We are not a passive people. Sometimes we have to fight in order to defend ourselves, as we did then.

---

[9] See note 8 above.
[10] Zohar 2, 161b.

Q: Does this relate to your military experience?

Deborah: Yes. The Canaanites were building up their forces to the north, and their threat was growing daily. As the tension mounted along our border, my husband, who had become more politically active, became a commander of troops. I asked him to summon our forces and form an alliance with the other Israelite tribes. It was clear that we needed to engage in a pre-emptive strike in order to protect our country.

Q: Pre-emptive strikes are used, though highly contested, in the twenty-first century.

Deborah: In that case, I hope that you have prophets who can balance wisdom and caution before battle, because a pre-emptive strike can be seen as an unwarranted act of aggression.

Q: Well, the enemy will always call it unjustifiable aggression, won't they?

Deborah: Yes. But the truth will surface sooner or later.

In the urgency to prevent an imminent attack, I told my husband that it was time for him to lead his soldiers to war, but he refused to leave without me. For this, some call him weak. But he knew that, given my prominence as a leader, our people would be less fearful if I was there. So I agreed to accompany him, and he turned out to be right. Prophets often went with the troops to inspire them and aid in the decision of when to fight.[11] War was usually considered a man's domain, but as a prophet and leader, my place was with my people.

Q: It sounds as though your husband did not feel threatened by your strength, but rather was secure in his own identity. Was it so easy for a woman to take on a man's role?

Deborah: Roles were less defined in my time. If a woman was qualified, she got the job. I took this job – and yet, if my husband was not to lead the military operation, then he would not win the

---

[11] *Reading the Women of the Bible*, 48.

laurels gained in victory. That honor would go to the woman who did. Isn't that fair?

Q: That goes without saying. You are fearless.[12]

Deborah: Of course, I had the private angst and fear that leaders can't reveal in public life. Prophets suffer from doubt too, and they often struggle for clarity and vision in turbulent times. I had to appear strong for the purpose of the mission, and I truly believed that I was saving and strengthening Israel. This is what made me a firebrand.

Q: Tell us about your victory.

Deborah: I devised a brilliant plan that helped us to defeat the enemy. Yet once the enemy troops were routed, their commander, Sisera, was still alive — and still a threat. This is where the story of Yael comes in. She lured him into her tent and killed him. I wrote of her in my victory song, "Blessed be Yael above all women."[13] You might wish to speak to her one day. She can tell you about her commitment to justice and the Jewish people. She was the bravest, strongest woman I have ever known.

Q: Then was it you or Yael who was the hero?

Deborah: It was Yael, no contest. Not many people could do what she did.

Q: You wrote a victory song that is now an entire chapter of the Book of Judges. Some say that it is full of conceit, while others say that it is cruel to your enemy.

Deborah: My song can be compared to the song that Moses and the Israelites sang at the Red Sea after they had crossed it and seen their enemy drowned. Both songs are victory chants that include praise and gratitude to God. One could say Moses was more modest than I, but I could not refrain from including myself

---

[12] *Biblical Images,* 2004.
[13] Judges 5:24.

in my song. I refer to myself as a mother in Israel and as a military leader. Perhaps some people might see that as ironic.

Q: By describing yourself as a mother in the midst of a military victory, what were you saying about motherhood? Were you saying that mothers are like military leaders – defending, supporting, working out strategy, protecting? Or were you commenting that military leaders should be tempered by the compassion of motherhood? Why did you mention the two roles together?

Deborah: Mothers *do* all these things – defend, support, work out strategy, protect and inspire. Perhaps I was saying that I felt the responsibility for the future of our people in the same way that a mother does for her children – and that was my primary role. I should have been introduced as a mother first.

Q: Tell us about your song.

Deborah: When the Jewish nation survived a pivotal event in their history, it was often recorded as a song or poem to express their gratitude. There are ten such songs in the Bible. In my song, I also settled many accounts, praising those who rallied to the cause and chastising those who did not. But above all, I praised God, Who, we believed, helped turn events in our favor even though we were so highly outnumbered by the enemy.

Q: Israel had a similar experience in the Six Day War many centuries later. Although it was surrounded and greatly outnumbered by its enemies, it was miraculously victorious.

Deborah: Where do you think our strength comes from, if not from our connection to the Creator of all things?

Q: Your faith is unbreakable!

In your song, your description of the enemy Sisera's mother is sensitive, empathetic, but chilling.

> Through the window she looked forth and peered, The mother of Sisera, through the lattice: "Why is his chariot so long in coming? Why tarry the wheels of his chariots?" The wisest of her princesses answer her, yea, she returneth

answer to herself: "Are they not finding, are they not dividing the spoil? A damsel, two damsels to every man; To Sisera a spoil of dyed garments, A spoil of dyed garments of embroidery, Two dyed garments of broidery for the neck of every spoiler?"[14]

Only one mother could describe another waiting for her son to return, the reader knowing he is never to return, with such poignancy. Again, motherhood is part of battle.

Deborah: I have no sympathy for evil or for those who would destroy others for the sake of their own power and glory. They must be dealt with harshly. As a mother, I wrote what I felt. I wrote about Sisera's mother's fear and yearning to see her son, but I had no pity for her. She was responsible for raising her son to be a vicious and cruel leader.

Q: Your convictions are forceful.

Deborah: There is a distinction between the holy and the profane, between that which is sanctified and that which is sullied. We were given the task to sanctify life and bring harmony to the world. If I have one obsession, it is to strive for these goals in all I do.

Q: How would you describe your unique mark as a hero of your time – your epitaph?

Deborah: An ethical action hero! My military strategy united the tribes of Israel for the first time in many years. Thus began a spirit of cooperation between the tribes in which the country was at peace for forty years. The Canaanites were no longer a threat.[15] Shortly afterwards, Ruth appeared, and only several generations later, through her lineage, Israel would crown its first king.

---

[14] Judges 5:28–30.
[15] Adin Steinsaltz, *Biblical Images: Men and Women of the Book*. New York: Basic Books, 1984, 105.

RUTH

RUTH WAS A MOABITE whose homeland is present-day Jordan, bordering on Israel. The Jewish people were forbidden to have anything to do with the people of Moab, as described in the Torah: "You shall not seek their peace or welfare all your days, forever, because they did not greet you with bread and water on the road when you were leaving Egypt, and because he hired against you Balaam... to curse you."[1] Yet Ruth, a Moabite woman, is a Jewish hero and a book of the Bible is named for her.[2] How can this be?

The Book of Ruth begins as follows: "It happened in the days when the Judges judged"[3] – a period of moral decay in the land of Israel, when the leaders earned neither the respect nor allegiance of the people. The year is approximately 1050 B.C.E. A famine is raging, society is floundering and the people are asking leaders such as the prophet Samuel for a king. As yet there is no established monarchy, and "every man [does] what was right in his own eyes."[4]

Some say that Ruth's story, which emerges from these troubled times, was recorded by the prophet Samuel. To this day, it is read in synagogues on the holiday of Shavuot, one of three primary holidays in the Jewish calendar. How did a book about a young woman who came from a nation that was forbidden to marry into the Jewish people come to be a central Jewish text? What did Ruth do to earn the high status that she eventually received?

Although Ruth's story takes place mainly in Bethlehem, the manner in which she arrived there is the axis of her extraordinary character. She leaves her family, her community and her country to

---

[1] Deuteronomy 23:4–7.
[2] *Jewish Literacy*, 23–25.
[3] Ruth 1:1.
[4] Judges 21:25.

adopt a new faith, joining a new community, and a new family. She clings to high ideals and becomes an example of how to live by them. The same Hebrew root, *d-v-k,* that the book of Ruth uses to describe her "clinging" to Naomi, her mother-in-law, is the same word that occurs in the Creation story, which describes how a man shall leave his parents and "cling" to his wife. In this case, the word means "to become one mind, one heart, one soul."[5] By clinging to her mother-in-law, Naomi, Ruth attained to great heights.

Her story is as follows: A wealthy man named Elimelech, who lives in Bethlehem, decides to leave the land of Israel. He takes his wife, Naomi, and his two sons to neighboring Moab. There Elimelech dies, and his sons marry Moabite women, Ruth and Orpah. Then the two sons die, leaving Naomi alone with her two childless Moabite daughters-in-law. Naomi decides to return to Bethlehem, and tells Ruth and Orpah to return to their families of origin so that they can go on with their lives. Orpah agrees but Ruth refuses, accompanying her mother-in-law to Bethlehem.

When they arrive there, it is the time of the barley harvest. In order to get food for herself and for Naomi, Ruth goes out to the fields to glean what the harvesters have left. The field she gathers food in belongs to a man named Boaz, who happens to be a relative of her late father-in-law. Boaz shows kindness to Ruth, having heard about her kindness and loyalty to Naomi.

The twist in the story comes in the form of an ancient custom of levirate marriage.[6] In this case, Boaz was a potential husband for Ruth by levirate marriage, since he was a surviving relative of Elimelech. Another twist appears when a man who is closer kin to Elimelech than Boaz is offered the opportunity to marry Ruth, but declines, allowing Boaz to take her as his wife.

---

[5] Rabbi Samson Raphael Hirsch's commentary on Genesis 2:24 in *The Stone Edition of The Chumash.*

[6] Wikipedia (online source), synopsis of Book of Ruth. For more on levirate marriage, see the story of Tamar, above.

Boaz and Ruth marry and have a son, Obed. The story concludes by tracing Obed's genealogy back to Judah, the son of Jacob, and into the future, in which Obed becomes the grandfather of King David.[7] Ruth, originally a member of the despised and forbidden Moabite nation, becomes King David's great-grandmother.

The following conversation between Ruth and Naomi sheds further light on the story.

RUTH: NAOMI, I have been meaning to ask you how you felt when your husband, Elimelech, decided to leave Israel and come to Moab. How did the people around you respond to his decision? After all, he could have helped them during the famine and evidently chose not to. Also, Jews were forbidden to marry Moabites. As I understand, the Jewish people considered Moab a nation of low morals and our women bad influences. Surely Elimelech knew his two unmarried sons would likely marry Moabites! What did you tell him? Did you have any say in the matter at all?

Naomi: Elimelech was a strong and prominent man in our community. As his wife, I followed him even though I knew it was wrong for us to go to Moab. I was young and didn't believe that I could be right and he, wrong. When the drought struck Bethlehem, my husband abandoned our people. We were wealthy and could have helped them, but Elimelech insisted on leaving. I feared the consequences – and sure enough, I lost everything: my husband, my sons, and everything we had. I believed at the time that God was punishing me.

Ruth: But things worked out in the end, didn't they? We stuck together and I gave you a beautiful grandson.

Naomi: *Someone* had a plan for us.

---

[7] Ruth 4:17–22.

Ruth: When you decided to return to Israel with a Moabite daughter-in-law in tow, you showed great strength and determination.

Naomi: I never knew I had such strength. When my husband and sons died, I was alone for the first time in my life. I felt guilty for not having protested when we left Israel, and I felt that I needed to atone somehow for having left. I saw nothing left in my life, and I wanted to die among my own people. I gathered all the energy and courage I had to make the move. At the time, Ruth, I was sure that you were coming with me out of pity.

Ruth: Not a bit of it! You had treated Orpah and me as daughters. You even called us "my daughters,"[8] remember? You showed us more respect than we had ever received from our own people, who saw us as chattels to be married off for material gain. But you cared about us. And when we lost our husbands, your sons, you still cared about our future, to the point that you urged us to return home, where we would be more comfortable, where we could remarry and build new lives again. But I felt closer to you than I ever did to my own mother. I had never experienced such kindness. People like you were rare in Moab.

Naomi: But there was no reason to come with me other than the feeling you describe. I had nothing to offer you. Orpah had every reason to return to her family. You were both exceptional to have married Jews, but Orpah did what most people in her situation would have done and returned to her community. But you, Ruth – you were stubborn! I'm not sure why you were so different, but it took courage for you to come with me. Did you want to prove to the Jews that they were too harsh in judging a whole nation as evil? After all, you showed that even a Moabite is capable of healing the

---

[8] Ruth 1:11.

world.[9] Were you embarrassed for your people? Where did you learn such lovingkindness?

Ruth: Before you came, my life was empty. I had few options. True, I led a privileged life as the daughter of King Eglon in Moab.[10] I had everything, but I had nothing. I was full of energy but had nowhere to direct it, since life in the palace was centered on the material world.

Then I met you, and suddenly everything was different. Your essence embodied what I was longing for: lovingkindness, spirituality, loyalty. Throughout all your challenges, life still kept its meaning for you. You lived by traditions that put family and relationships first. I loved that, and I began to experience it in my marriage to your son.

Naomi: And this feeling was enough for you to leave everything and risk your family's anger by going off with an Israelite?

Ruth: Naomi, you say that I had courage, but you had much more. Although you were utterly alone, you chose to return to Israel. All I had was an instinct that drew me to cling to you. Finally, I realized that I, too, could right a wrong – in our common history, my people's wrongs to yours.

Naomi: Ruth, I admire you for not succumbing to the emptiness in your life. You never gave up hope that things could be better. That is tenacity. People like you who hear their inner voice, wait until there is clarity and use an opportunity to change. All too many people hear that voice and ignore it. You listened.

Ruth: When I look back, it seems that I was yearning for spirituality and was attracted to yours. Even "in [your] loneliness

---

[9] *Megillat Ruth: Hesed and Hutzpah, A Literary Approach.* Study Guide by Noam Zion. Shalom Hartman Institute, Tichon Seminar, 2005, 4.

[10] *The Book of Ruth.* Artscroll Tanach Series. New York: Mesorah Publications, 1990, 67.

and fear, in [your] emptiness and widowhood... you were tied to Torah."[11] You said the values that guided you came from your God, and I needed to learn more. Your religion seemed honest and truthful. I would have done anything for you.

Naomi: The words that you said when you decided to remain with me are immortal. When I tried to persuade you to return to your home, you said: "Wherever you go, I will go; where you lodge, I will lodge. Your people are my people, and your God is my God. Where you die, I will die, and there I will be buried."[12] You have become an immortal paradigm of loyalty to the God of Israel. You should be proud.

Ruth: My words were spontaneous, the result of years of yearning. It is as if they had been stored inside me, waiting to be said. You, Naomi, introduced me to the God of Israel and I had no trouble believing.

Naomi: The Book of Ruth is read on Shavuot, when we commemorate the giving of the Torah on Mount Sinai. You have an excellent place in the Jewish calendar.

Ruth: We arrived in Bethlehem, Israel during the gathering of the first fruits, which coincides with the date on which the Jews received the Torah at Mount Sinai, seven weeks after they had left Egypt. The timing and subject of my story is about all these elements – the harvest, acceptance of God's law, and gratitude. For all these reasons, the book named for me is read on the holiday.

Although we were poor and hungry when we returned to Israel, we benefited from landowners who left a generous part of their harvest on the ground for those like us, who had nothing. According to the law, we were allowed to take the odd sheaves that had been overlooked or left by harvesters. We could take from the corners of fields, which were not allowed to be harvest, and we

---

[11] Zion, Noam. *Megillat Ruth – Hesed and Hutzpah: A Literary Approach.* Study guide, Shalom Hartman Institute.
[12] Ruth 1:16–17.

could take whatever the harvesters individually dropped, since they were not allowed to go back and pick it up. The Israelites had already created a system of charity and we were grateful.

Naomi: It's hard for me to think back on those days. When I returned to Bethlehem, I was a changed woman. Even my old friends didn't recognize me. I must have aged terribly. I had left as a woman of status and returned a poor migrant. As if all that weren't enough, I was coming back with a Moabite woman.

My troubles were so great that I felt I had nothing to lose. As I saw it, things could not get any worse, and I no longer cared what others might think. I had to survive and take care of you as best I could. Also, as I reflected that I had nothing more to lose, I began to feel rebellious.[13]

Ruth: Yes. In Bethlehem you were not the warm, loving woman I first knew. You were angry with those who welcomed you, and you were angry with God. But you still cared for me and thought of my future, if not yours.

Naomi: I'm sorry I was of no comfort to you. You were so loyal to me, and yet you must have felt lonely and homesick yourself. Weren't you afraid that people might harm you if they knew where you were from? And yet you went out every day to glean by yourself. Your instinct to be kind and caring was strong, exactly as if you had been a Jew all your life.

Ruth: When I went out to the fields to glean, I could only think of sharing and eating with you at the end of the day when you would teach me more about Torah and a God with whom you could be angry!

Naomi: You are extraordinary.

---

[13] Zornberg, Avivah. "The Concealed Alternative." In *Megillat Ruth: Hesed and Hutzpah, A Literary Approach*. Study Guide by Noam Zion. Shalom Hartman Institute, Tichon Seminar, 2005, 48–55.

Ruth: Only because I learned from you. Eventually I came to believe that it was God, not luck, Who put me in the fields of Boaz.

Naomi: It was. We don't believe in luck. We believe in happenings – fate – "those moments in life that we don't direct but which direct us – events that are unexpected, not intended, but which all the more could be the most *intentional* messages sent by the One Who directs and brings about all things."[14]

Ruth: There is something I have wondered for some time. I was frightened when I went out to glean that first day, hoping to find a landowner who would allow a single woman to collect enough for us both.[15] Why didn't you tell me that you had a relative who had many fields near where we had settled?

Naomi: I felt humiliated, and I was ashamed of my situation. I felt too guilty, too responsible for the deaths of Elimelech and my sons, to contact our cousin Boaz or to reach out to family. But sometimes I wonder why Boaz did not come to me. He knew that I had returned with a young daughter-in-law. He had heard that I returned poor and hungry. Only once he met you did he seem to be kind. You awakened something in him so that he, too, became extraordinary in kindness.[16] You and our ancestor Tamar, who was also from a neighboring country, "called an Israelite man to responsibility."[17]

Ruth: Going for the good always has its rewards.

Naomi: Our story ended well. When you gave birth to your son, Obed, and our neighbors came to bless me, too, I could no longer be angry with God. I felt hopeful and full, and now I blessed God.[18] You made me so proud, as an example of how an outsider

---

14 *The Book of Ruth.* Artscroll Series, Commentary by Rabbi Samson Raphael Hirsch, 88.

15 Ruth 2:1–3.

16 *Megillat Ruth: Hesed and Hutzpah,* 48.

17 *Megillat Ruth: Hesed and Hutzpah,* 89.

18 Ibid., 79.

can be a shining example of Judaism's essence. The Jewish monarchy sprung from you.

Our sages say that God holds a special love for converts because they come to Judaism of their own volition.[19]

Ruth: I was given the opportunity to go beyond what I was born into, beyond duty. That is called *hesed*. I also had *hutzpah* – that's doing the extraordinary. It's not so hard to show *hesed* every day. It's harder to be extraordinary, but it's always good to keep a lookout for those occasions when we *can* be.

---

[19] Ibid., 32.

ESTHER

THE JEWISH HOLIDAY of Purim, which occurs in late winter or early spring, celebrates an occasion on which Jews who lived outside Israel overcame anti-Semitism and affirmed their future. The original story for this holiday took place in the fourth century B.C.E. when the Jews of Persia – present-day Iran – were in danger of being annihilated. Like the Jews in Europe twenty-five centuries later, they were targeted for destruction simply because they were Jews.

How did Jews get to Persia from Israel? In 586 B.C.E., approximately fifty years previously, the Temple in Jerusalem was destroyed, together with the Jewish state. Jews fled en masse and settled in the neighboring Persian Empire, where the Purim story takes place.

The Purim story is recorded in the Book of Esther, which is included in the larger body of canonized Jewish texts known as the Tanach.

Jewish ritual mandates that Jews gather on the fourteenth day of the Hebrew month of Adar[1] in order to hear the Book of Esther read. They then share a meal that commemorates the Jews' victory over those who sought to destroy them.

The story of Purim is very much loved because its ending is positive and its message uplifting. It teaches us that although fate can be unpredictable and cruel, we can create happy endings and turn tragedy to joy. Esther's story is an example of the difference between fate and destiny. The modern Jewish philosopher, Rabbi

---

[1] In the case of an ancient walled city, the gathering takes place on the fifteenth day of Adar. Esther 9:18–19.

Joseph Soloveitchik, said, "God may decide our fate, but we determine our destiny."[2]

Esther, the heroine of the Purim story, is a descendant of Benjamin, the son of Rachel and Jacob. Esther grew up knowing two basic things about herself: she was Jewish, and she was attractive. She matured into a woman who understood not only her feminine power but also the importance of Jewish memory. Esther is the paradigm of one who transforms herself from just another pretty face to a woman who is able to take charge. She used subtlety, charm, good timing, and stealth to save her people. In her story, circumstance stirred vague Jewish memories from her childhood and she rediscovered the importance of loyalty, faith, prayer, and action. She also realized that each one of us is responsible for the survival of Judaism. This is the strongest message of her story.

Esther also shows us how to imbue wealth and privilege with meaning. In her case, she recognized that in the royal culture she lived, her beauty and sexuality were forms of power. Tamar Frankiel, an American Jewish scholar, aptly observed: "At first, Esther did not know how her personal assets would eventually bring her to a heroic opportunity.... But she, and Mordechai, knew or sensed where her power lay, and she protected it even to the point of hiding her Jewish identity."[3] Esther kept her identity as a Jew hidden until she had enough power to act to save her people.

Esther also reminds us that "everyone, man or woman, has a mission in life which he or she has to accept, and that every member of the People of Israel has a duty to preserve the existence of the people by the means available to him or her."[4] Although she is the paradigm of the assimilated Diaspora Jew, when she

---

[2] Soloveitchik, Rabbi Joseph B. *Fate and Destiny*. New Jersey: Ktav Publishing House, 1992.

[3] *The Voice of Sarah*, 30–31.

[4] *Feminine Aspects of Megillat Esther*. Jewish Agency for Israel, Department of Jewish Zionist Education. Purim, 2004. Accessible at www.jafi.org.il/education.

experienced her "Sinaitic moment" – the instant in time when she realized what she must do – she rose to the challenge. She then saved her people by using inner strength that she never knew she had.

Also hidden in her story, never mentioned directly, is God. According to the sages, God withdraws from us in the same measure that we do from Him. The Divine was hidden, as were Esther's identity and her power to redeem, until she showed us that coincidences and luck are miracles and signs when we see them as such. From a secular, fully assimilated Jew coddled in affluence, Esther emerged as a full working partner with God. On Purim, "we celebrate not only the survival of our ancestors, but the assertiveness of their queen," according to the modern author, Letty Cottin Pogrebin.[5] We rejoice over Jewish success – not in defeating others, but in survival. We then show our gratitude in joy and celebration.

The sages also say that only when Esther's generation emerged from assimilation, taking full responsibility for their Jewish identity, did the Jewish nation become complete partners in the covenant of Sinai.[6]

Q: WELCOME, Queen Esther.

Esther: Please, just call me Esther. It's my Persian name. My Jewish name is Hadassah. Our parents gave us popular Persian names along with our Jewish ones.

Q: We do the same. But most of us don't use our Jewish names.

Esther: (smiling) You see? That is one thing we already share.

Q: Tell us when and how you lived.

Esther: I grew up in my Uncle Mordechai's home in Shushan, the capital of the Persian Empire. My parents died when I was very

---

[5] Pogrebin, Letty Cottin. *Deborah, Golda, and Me.* New York: Crown Publishers, 1991, 135.

[6] *Shabbat* 88a.

young and I was adopted by extended family. I was very beautiful, an important asset for an orphan.

Q: What do you mean?

Esther: When you're beautiful, you get attention. People used to tell me, "You're such a beauty, little Esther. Your skin is so perfect. Your hair is like silk." I paid attention.

I never heard my family talk about who should take care of me, but thank God I ended up with my uncle Mordechai, who lived alone but had money and a large house. Mordechai was one of my quieter relatives. I clung to him, since I sensed somehow that he loved me rather than pitied me.

Q: You must have loved him too.

Esther: Oh, I did! Uncle Mordechai raised me as his daughter and gave me everything. He was a learned Jew who also played an important part in Persian society. We often felt more Persian than Jewish, you know. When times were good, it would have been difficult for us and most Jews in Shushan to choose where our loyalties lay.

Q: This is a familiar topic in North America today.

Esther: Jews do well as long as their host country treats them fairly. But things can go badly, even if you can't imagine it happening in your day. Now that the modern State of Israel exists, thank God, Jews again have a home of their own. In my day, there was no Jewish country. We had been driven into exile before I was born.

My family could trace its roots to Saul, the first king of Israel, who lived about five hundred years before us and reigned just before the first great Temple was built in Jerusalem. At that time, Israel was the home of all Jews. I clung to my royal roots proudly, even though in Persia they meant nothing. I was captivated and enchanted by anything royal. Since Uncle Mordechai was the accountant for the Persian royal family, I knew all about Persian royalty.

The royal palace in Shushan was the headquarters of the king, his government and his family. It sat on top of the highest hill in the center of the city. The front gate leading to it was magnificent – each portal was two stories high and was elaborately decorated with scrolls made from wrought iron intertwined with clusters of fruits in gold and silver. When both gates were open, chariots could pass through four abreast. When they were closed, one could still catch a glimpse of the inner courtyards and, if one was lucky, of the queen or the king as well.

A large public square surrounded the palace entrance and sloped down the hill to the shops and neighborhoods below. The neighborhoods near the square were the nicest, of course and that's where we lived. The streets were clean and the gates to the common homes were also decorated in wrought iron. It was a quiet neighborhood, much quieter than the ones that spread down toward the markets and the outer city walls.

Uncle Mordechai gave me as much love and attention as he could. Although he often worked late, he would always wake me to tell me he loved me, his beautiful princess. He never realized that I always waited for him to come home before I could fall asleep. He brought home pomegranates, my favorite fruit for breakfast, every day when they were in season.

I had the best guardians and tutors that Uncle Mordechai could find for me. But there is no word for the loneliness of a child who has no mother. My imagination kept me going as I made elaborate tea parties and banquets with "babysitters-in-waiting." A silk scarf thrown on a bench served as a tablecloth for my miniature tea set. We ate cakes with milk and I, of course, was always the queen. I imagined that my mother and father sat at the table with me, telling stories of my babyhood. "You were such a beautiful and happy baby," I would imagine my mother saying. In my mind, my father would laugh and recall how he had to beg her to let him hold me for a few moments. In my mind, they were loving and perfect parents.

(As I watch, Esther gently tugs a beautiful silk scarf from her shoulders, waving it high in the air until it floats to the center of our table. It is the color of the sea, purple and blue, crowned by a gold crest of scrolls, lions, and vines, all intertwined. Her eyes focus on a place that only she can see. Her expression is wistful, as if she wished to return once more to that place of comfort – her parents' love.)

As I grew, so did my love for royalty and drama. I charmed my way into every leading role in every play that my friends and I put on. I loved to weave my uncle's stories of palace intrigues into our scripts. "Did you hear that the queen didn't wear the right crown to the feast last night? The king was so angry that he had the wardrobe mistress thrown into the dungeon!"

Or: "Did you know the king wants to shuffle his advisors again? Whom will he dismiss this time? Who will be the new advisers?" All this storytelling helped me cope with my constant sadness.

I also loved fashion. I would beg my uncle to have seamstresses sew me outfit after outfit. I would wheedle my uncle: "Please, Uncle Mordechai, if you buy me two and a half meters of mauve silk with some lavender lace for the collar and cuffs, the seamstress will make me the most gorgeous skirt and tunic for the holidays, and then I can wear it again when you bring me to the palace. I'll make you so proud!" I always had reason for a new outfit. I had to be striking, not just beautiful. The more attention from these clothes and my good looks, the better I felt.

Q: You sound like many girls today.

Esther: Maybe… but I hope that they are not as lonely as I was. I would have given anything to have parents to hug me, even to argue with me. If I could have spent time with my mother, learning from her, going out with her, talking to her, then perhaps I wouldn't have needed so many material things.

Q: Is that something mothers should think about?

Esther: Girls in Shushan had tutors in the morning for Persian arts and culture. Since afternoons were free, I spent most of those at my girlfriends' homes, competing for their mothers' attention. My governesses were good to me. They really did care for me, but I kept everyone at a distance. Actually, I really *am* a warm person, but no one could fill the role of my perfect imaginary mother. So I came across as difficult and rude.

When I was feeling upset – which was more often than I like to admit – I would snap, "Stay away from me! You don't understand and you never will, so don't say that you do!" I guess I wasn't an easy child, but they tried their best.

When my uncle taught me stories of women in Jewish tradition, I imagined my mother to have been them all – strong like Sarah, brave and daring like Tamar, clever like Rebecca, beloved like Rachel, and a prophet and visionary like Miriam. In my imagination, there were no limitations to my mother's greatness. No one could possibly live up to her.

As a teenager, Mordechai also taught me about the Jewish leaders in Jerusalem who were known as the prophets. Teachers traveled at great risk to spread the messages of the prophets to Jews like us, who lived assimilated lives in the Diaspora. They quoted the prophet Hosea – "There is no truth, nor mercy, nor knowledge of God in the land... therefore doth the land mourn."[7] And they quoted the prophet Joel – "Whosoever shall call on the name of the Lord shall be delivered; I will gather all nations and will bring them down into the valley of Jehoshaphat; for My people and for My heritage Israel, whom they have scattered among the nations and divided My land."[8] These teachers believed that by learning Torah, we could reclaim Israel, our homeland, and they exhorted us to become more pious and observant of Jewish custom. But my friends and I were too busy with clothes and gossip and intrigues of our own. Knowing that we were Jewish was enough for us.

Q: Now you really sound like an assimilated Diaspora Jew. Jewish observance is often secondary or neglected in modern life.

---

[7] Hosea 4:1–3.
[8] Joel 3:5–7, 4:2.

Esther: Yes. As I learned during my own girlhood, it is all too easy to distance ourselves from our roots. But now let me return to the palace.

Vashti was our queen. Her beauty was legendary, and whenever she appeared I noticed her every detail – the way she folded her hands, the way she held her head high, though not in a haughty manner, her chin just parallel to the ground, strong and forward. She was royalty and dignity personified. For me, she was yet another of my imaginary mothers.

One night, during the third year of our king's reign, he held a great feast for all his nobles from all over the Empire. At one point, when everyone had gotten more than a little drunk, the king took it into his head to show them all how beautiful his wife was. He summoned Vashti, telling her to appear before them all wearing her royal crown – and according to some of the officials who were at the feast, he actually ordered her to appear wearing *only* her royal crown and nothing else! Outraged by the king's order, Vashti refused to show herself before all those drunken men. Later, some of her women told me, in whispers, what she said that night.

"How could my husband order his own wife to display herself before all those men? And how could I possibly obey such an order? I am the Queen of the Persian Empire, not some harem slave bought at market! Those wicked advisers of his must have put him up to this. How could he listen to them? Has he no shame?

"I know that if I disobey him, he will divorce me, perhaps even kill me. But I will not, I cannot do what he asks. The dignity of the queen is the dignity of the Empire. It must never be compromised." She turned to the servants who had brought her the order and said, "Tell the king's chamberlains that Queen Vashti regrets that she cannot appear before the king at this time." Her maids said that her face was pale and she trembled as she spoke. Yet although she was terrified, she stuck to her decision.

Of course, the king was furious. On the advice of his ministers, he stripped Vashti of her rank as queen and divorced her. This was supposed to set an example to all women lest they, too, think of disobeying their husbands.

It was the last anyone ever heard of her. The only official word from the palace was that Vashti was no longer queen. Whether she was banished from the palace, thrown into prison, relegated to some forgotten corner of the harem or even executed, we never knew. I was devastated. I had idolized Vashti and daydreamed that I might be like her one day.

What she did took tremendous courage, but it was also tantamount to suicide. Even a commoner woman who disobeyed her husband ran a tremendous risk in those days. But that a queen should defy her husband before all his nobles – that could not be tolerated. So Vashti simply disappeared.

Q: Today we have places of refuge to protect and shelter women when they are abused.

Esther: That is a good thing, of course, but it is too bad that such a thing is necessary. Everyone talked about Vashti and what she had done for years, though in whispers, of course. No one could let the king or his officials know that they secretly sympathized with the deposed queen. Personally, I think that she qualifies as a heroine herself.

Q: So now the king had no queen.

Esther: Yes. And apparently I wasn't the only one who missed her. The king had loved Vashti and fell into a deep depression of anger and guilt over having dismissed her. He couldn't sleep. He cried. When he finally did get out of bed, he paced up and down the halls and walked circles in the courtyards, mumbling constantly to himself. His advisors began to be concerned about his erratic behavior and feared that the king might become insane and then turn on them. So they convinced him to find a new queen.

Q: And this is where you came in?

Esther: When Uncle Mordechai arrived home unusually early one afternoon, he came into my room as I was reading, and sat down on the edge of my bed. I knew there was something important on his mind. He looked at me, but his eyes narrowed and avoided mine. I started to feel a wave of dread in my heart as I sat up and put down my book. He told me that the king was searching throughout the kingdom for a new queen, and that all young women of marriageable age were summoned to the palace as candidates. He seemed to want me to go, which I thought was strange. But I listened anyway.

Q: How old were you?

Esther: I wasn't far into my teens then. That was the age when most girls married in our kingdom. Uncle Mordechai promised to keep close watch on me as business often brought him into the palace. I was frightened but I could not disobey. It was the king's own order. To disobey it would have meant ending up like Vashti – and no one was even certain what had happened to her.

Q: It appears that your uncle also wanted you to go. And you felt indebted to him – after all, he had raised you.

Esther: In our day, girls had limited choices and were dependent on the benevolence of their fathers or guardians. If we had any talent in the arts or for studies, then we could become artisans or teachers, but only in a sheltered, controlled way. The best that many of us could hope for was a loveless arranged marriage with an older man that would at least bring some financial security to us and perhaps to our families.

Q: You were chosen as the new queen. We are told that the king was in love with you.

Esther: Actually, we were both sad people, and each of us felt that in the other. We had sadness in common.

Q: What was Ahashverosh like?

Esther: He was usually engrossed in himself. He wasn't a strong man, physically or morally, and he was constantly overwhelmed. Men hovered at his shoulders, constantly whispering in his ears. At the selection banquet, he didn't take his eyes off me. Much later, he told me that he was thinking that this would be one decision he would make on his own.

Q: And you were Jewish. How did that play out?

Esther: Just before my coronation, in a moment alone with Uncle Mordechai, he held my face in his two hands, kissed my forehead, took my hands, and looked deeply into my eyes. He warned me to be careful to whom I talked and what I said, and never to trust anyone in the palace. He also told me never to let anyone know that I was a Jew. I did not even have time to be shocked. My uncle then stepped back, and I stepped up to the throne.

Q: You were surprised.

Esther: I was naïve, and Uncle Mordechai knew it. So began my double life. I was more sheltered and pampered than ever, but a good deal less safe. The palace banquets were no longer a young girl's fantasy. Oh, they were pleasant enough up to a point, but I could not help wondering what I was doing there. It seemed that my uncle had *wanted* me to become queen. Why? And what did my being Jewish have to do with it?

Q: Was it because now you had no choice but to hide the fact that you were Jewish?

Esther: I had never felt the importance of my Jewish identity until it was taken away. I began reminiscing about holidays and what I had learned about the Jewish people and its history. I frequently remembered our family gatherings, with their special Jewish foods. I recalled the stories from our tradition that I had been taught, particularly the story of Joseph, who also lived in a dictator's palace over a thousand years before me. I wished that I had learned more about him. He was luckier than I was because he didn't have to hide his being Jewish, and he had power. Joseph's story made me think that perhaps I could have power, too – at least enough to keep me safe.

Q: What were your greatest luxuries in the palace?

Esther: The best traders with the best goods came to the queen's palace first. I had the finest fabrics and silks in the world, with spectacular embroidery. We had court embroiderers whose only job was to stitch the most intricate details of nature, animals, or whatever design I desired. I still loved clothes, just as I had as a young girl. Now they provided me with an escape from reality.

My servants catered to me day and night. Before my bath every morning, I had a massage, a facial, manicure and pedicure. Of course, this was not only for me. A beautiful queen reflected well on the Empire, and on the king, my husband. Another luxury was my chariot. Ornate and spacious, it had a special inner chamber with a table at which I could eat and drink while traveling. The windows had special curtains that let me see out but allowed no one to see in. Two handsome stallions powered my carriage. They were tall and flaxen, and always held their heads high. They strutted and galloped with an energy of life that I envied.

Q: Were you involved in any of the workings of the palace?

Esther: No. I was an ornament on the King's arm, and my only job was to make him happy. My life was full of fuss and finery but devoid of meaning. I did not like this state of affairs at all, but I hid my discontent. I had to.

Q: It sounds like you were waiting for the Book of Esther to unfold.

Esther: I was ready for something. I began to keep track of the ministers and advisors and what they did. Slowly I learned about the kingdom's politics, power struggles and intrigues. Then, one morning several years after I had become queen, Uncle Mordechai sent me a message asking for an immediate audience. That was how things worked at the palace – I could not just go out to meet him! Of course, I agreed. When he arrived, he told me that two of the king's trusted servants were plotting to assassinate him, and I told my husband immediately. I also made sure that he knew who had saved him. Uncle Mordechai's name and loyal deed were recorded in the king's book of records. That was the first time that I used my power as queen. I felt my power, and I liked the feeling.

Q: How else did you use your power as queen?

Esther: I started making differences, first small ones and then larger ones, in palace life and in Persian society, through my influence with the king. Sometimes I would tell the king, over a good dinner: "My dearest lord, I heard the wife of the ambassador from the eastern provinces mention over lunch today that the roads there are in urgent need of repair." Or as we left the city to enjoy the fresh air of the countryside, I might ask him, "My lord and husband, what do you think would be the best way to improve waste disposal at the market?" He would answer, "An excellent idea, my beauty. I will tell my advisors to look into it, my love." And it would be done.

Q: That was a selfless way to use your power.

Esther: Well, I was no longer the spoiled little girl I had been. Now I was a mature young woman with responsibilities, and I had learned how to use my power in the palace for good purposes.

But one day, my chamberlains came to me with an urgent message: my uncle Mordechai was wearing sackcloth before the very palace gates! The news upset me terribly. No one was allowed to enter the palace wearing mourning clothes. It was unheard of! I had always known my uncle to be a level-headed man. He was not the sort to make such a display without good reason. I sent my chamberlain to ask my uncle what was wrong. Through him, Uncle Mordechai told me that the king had appointed a new chief advisor, a vicious man chosen principally to protect the King from future assassination attempts….

Q: That would be Haman. Am I correct?

Esther: Yes. The man was a snake, and it was well known that he hated Jews. Only a short time before, my husband had made him his chief adviser – the equivalent of his second-in-command over the entire Empire. I had tried to persuade Ahashverosh not to do it, but my efforts were unsuccessful. To make matters worse, once he had appointed Haman to this high position, he started seeking out my company less and less. I began to be concerned about our marriage, and about my position in the palace. I didn't want to go the same way as Vashti.

Q: We know that Mordechai made a point of refusing to bow down before Haman. Why provoke such a confrontation?

Esther: A Jew living under foreign rule may bow down to those in authority if he must.[9] But Haman was a known Jew-hater, and my uncle, a proud Jew, simply could not bring himself to do it.

Q: Why was your uncle in mourning before the very palace gates?

Esther: It turned out that Haman had persuaded my husband to sign a terrible decree. It allowed all the subjects of the Persian Empire to rise up against all its Jewish inhabitants on a given day, the fourteenth of Adar, kill them to the last man, woman and child, and take their property as plunder. I was stunned. For a moment I felt that I could understand Vashti's anger at Ahashverosh during the feast, on her last night as queen. How could the king even consider signing such a cruel decree? How could he be so foolish and hard-hearted? To kill innocent people without provocation, no matter who they are, is wrong! But these were my own people in mortal danger, and I, the queen, was a Jew myself. I was terrified. I didn't know what to do.

Q: What happened then?

Esther: Uncle Mordechai asked me to go to the king and use my influence with him to have the decree annulled. I explained that I could only go before the king if he summoned me, since there was a law in the kingdom that anyone, man or woman, who came before the king uninvited could be killed on the spot. And my husband had not summoned me to his presence for a whole month. I was already concerned about my future in the palace. If I went before Ahashverosh without his having summoned me, I might die before I had a chance to say a single word! How would this save our people?

Q: Yet you changed your mind and decided to go to him, knowing that you were risking your life. Why?

---

[9] *Bava Kamma* 113a. "Samuel said: The law of the land is binding law."

Esther: It was my instinct for Jewish survival. It was a matter of a moment, a *rega,* an instant during which I realized that I could change my own and my people's destiny.

Q: As someone who seized the moment and acted, do you think we are always just a moment away from something great?

Esther: Some pivotal moments may not be as obvious as others. Sometimes they appear as quiet threats, like assimilation. But yes, the tiniest instant can change our lives. And in one tiny instant, I decided to act. I had as much power as Joseph had, but in a different way. Although I did not succeed in getting Haman's decree annulled, I saved our people just the same. You can read how I did it in my book.

Q: Why is it so important to be Jewish? We can be good people no matter what our religion. We can be good people even without religion.

Esther: While other religions may concentrate on otherworldly matters, Judaism teaches us how to make this world a better place. Our heroes are flawed and human, like me, and their stories, like mine, involve real-life dilemmas in which we may fail, but this is part of the process of rising up once again with new strength, resolve, and commitment. A religion with heroes who are flawed but still good was a first in ancient times.[10]

Q: So what do you believe being a Jew is all about?

Esther: We are here to improve human life. Judaism believes in a God Who believes in us. No people before us ever chose to apply these values, and no people before us valued life with so much intensity. When Judaism first began, people were still sacrificing their children to gods whom they themselves saw as capricious, to idols of clay and stone. In their religions, there was barely any difference between natural forces and the free will of human beings. Their gods justified immoral and inconsistent behavior by engaging

---

[10] Soloveitchik, Rabbi Joseph B. *The Halakhic Mind.* New York: Seth Press, 1986.

in it themselves, removing all need for human responsibility and accountability. Judaism teaches us that while we can't explain everything, we must strive to improve ourselves in every relationship and circumstance that we may encounter. It does not allow us to use our power for selfish and violent ends.

So we may answer the question of why being Jewish is important with the vision of perfecting an imperfect world, as our ancestors and sages did.

Q: What inspired you in your own moment of crisis?

Esther: I thought of the prophet Joel and his idea of fasting as a way of invoking Divine help during periods of crisis in Jewish history. So I called upon all our people to fast and pray.

I also thought about the prophet Malachi's message about returning to God: "Return to Me and I will return to you."[11] This was my own story. I had been an assimilated Jew who returned to Judaism at a critical moment in my own life and in the life of my people.

Q: What message do you have for us today?

Esther: In my story, God does not have a starring role. People make it happen. Unlike in the Bible, God appears to be absent in my book. In fact, no Divine name is ever mentioned. But we believe that God's hand is always there when we extend ours. The rebuilding of Israel and the construction of the Second Temple began soon after my story, and the Book of Esther is the last book of the Bible. I would like to believe that the original festival of Purim was a paradigm for commitment and action.

Q: When we celebrate Purim today, most little girls dress up as Queen Esther. Which of your characteristics should they be honoring?[12]

---

[11] Malachi 3:7.

[12] *Teachings on Esther.* Shalom Hartman Institute, Jerusalem, Israel, www.hartman.org.il.

Esther: The little girl who dresses up as me on Purim can change the world, too. She has her own power, and we can help her to become a loyal member of the Jewish people by giving her as many pleasant Jewish memories as possible.

Q: One last question. How did costume and masks come to symbolize Purim?

Esther: There are many answers to that question. One is that there is a fine line between what is and what can be, what and who are real and are not real. If you hide behind a mask of indifference or fear, opportunities will pass you by. If you assume the mask of a hero or role model, then in a *rega,* an instant, you can become who you never thought you could be. The real threat to Jewish survival may be in hiding behind a mask of complacency. Still another answer may be that Purim celebrates a hidden God until such time as we are ready to acknowledge the Divine openly in our lives.

I became the activist I never thought I could be. Life can be topsy-turvy. Visions can change. Once again, I am thinking of the prophet Joel, who said, "The old shall dream dreams, the young shall see visions."[13] What are the visions that people have today?

I would like to suggest putting on a mask adorned with the precious jewels of our history and linking yourself to the chain of Jewish heroes just by thinking that you can. And then we will all say: Amen!

---

[13] Joel 3:1.

RACHEL, WIFE OF AKIVA

ONE COULD SAY that Rachel is the one who discovered Rabbi Akiva, whose life-support techniques kept Judaism alive during the time of the destruction of the second Temple in Jerusalem in 70 C.E. by the Romans and Israel's subsequent loss of statehood.

As a result of the destruction of Israel, Jews fled to a variety of neighboring countries, but those that remained were fragmented throughout the land, dominated by foreign rule for centuries until the Modern State of Israel was established in 1948 C.E., almost two thousand years later.

Let us backtrack briefly to an overview of the formation of the Jewish nation up to the time of Akiva and Rachel.

After leaving Egypt, the Israelites traveled through the desert, led by Moses, where they encountered God at Mount Sinai. There they accepted the foundations of their belief, the Ten Commandments, which identified them as a nation that would strive to live by its principles and merit to acquire the land of Israel as its homeland.

Although Moses had led the Israelites through their birth as a nation, he died before he could enter Israel, passing the mantle of leadership to Joshua bin Nun. Under Joshua, the Jews possessed the land and settled there. For more than six hundred years, the Jews in Israel thrived under a series of kingships in which their religion and culture were deepened by judges, prophets and leaders, all of whom added layers of meaning to the original stories in their history. During the reign of King Solomon, who succeeded his father, King David, the first great Temple in Jerusalem was built, which became the epitome of the glory of Jewish life. People went there in order to worship, show gratitude to God, atone for sins, learn, and do business. They celebrated the cycles of life and nature, and came to be one with their God.

After King Solomon's reign, aspirations of political and material gain seeped into Jewish leadership, and the bonds of Jewish wisdom and faith that had elevated Jewish life began to disintegrate. Corruption and infighting weakened the nation. Eventually, the Babylonians destroyed the Temple and exiled the Israelites in 586 B.C.E. Most of the Israelites fled to Babylonia (present-day Iraq) and Persia (present-day Iran), where they managed to stay together as a community. Then, thanks to heroes like Esther and to the beneficence of enlightened foreign rulers such as King Cyrus of Persia, the Israelites returned to Jerusalem and built another Temple there in 520 B.C.E. Many of the Israelites returned, reclaimed their land and thrived, although divisiveness and strife remained in their community. Centuries later, in approximately 165 B.C.E., the Syrian-Greeks under King Antiochus Epiphanes invaded and took over the Temple, but the Jews fought back and won. Their victory became the celebration of the first Hanukkah. Although the Temple remained standing, a century later, the Romans invaded. The Jews tried to fight back, but this time they were unsuccessful, and in 70 C.E. the Romans destroyed the Second Temple and exiled those Jews who had survived the battles and siege, dispersing them throughout the known world.

What did this mean for Jewish survival? How could the Jews keep their faith alive when their nation was dispersed and broken? During this time, Jewish scholars known as the sages taught and interpreted Jewish law.[1] Discussions at the various academies of Jewish learning centered on the practice and laws of Judaism and decided which texts would be included in the Jewish canon, known as the Tanach.[2]

---

[1] Encarta online Jewish dictionary.

[2] The Tanach – the Jewish canon of the Written Law – includes the Pentateuch, the early Prophets, the later Prophets, and the Hagiographa. This latter section of the Tanach, which is also known as the Writings, includes the books of Psalms, Proverbs, Job, the Song of Songs, Ruth, Lamentations, Ecclesiastes, Esther, Daniel, Ezra, Nehemiah, and First and Second Chronicles.

This was a fractious time, when rival personalities vied for credibility opposite the Sanhedrin, which remained the final authority in Jewish matters. The debates among the Jewish leaders often centered on the dilemma of compliance to Roman edicts that violated Jewish law versus Jewish survival. Secrecy was the order of the day as Jews tried once again to survive as a nation without a land – the only nation to endure this way throughout history.

The conquest of Jerusalem was a great victory for the Romans. The Jews were exiled and enslaved. Families and communities were torn apart. While some had managed to flee before the invasion, thousands were killed by the Roman army, which raided neighborhoods throughout Israel. Others survived by hiding or by bribery. When the battle was over, those who chose to stay in Israel lived under great suppression and hardship imposed by Roman rule. The mood was fraught with fear and despair. Some of those who stayed still hoped to rebel against the Romans and restore Jewish independence.

It was during this tumultuous time that Rachel lived in Jerusalem, not far from the ruins of the Temple. Judaism was about to take a sharp turn off the course it had known for almost thirteen centuries, but through a stroke of love and instinctual wisdom, Rachel, the daughter of a wealthy man named Joshua, saw the hidden light and brilliance in a shepherd named Akiva ben Joseph. Through her love and sacrifice, the shepherd Akiva became a great rabbi who transformed the Jewish world and prepared it for its future. Rachel, the wife of Akiva, is the true sister of all women who perform the random, hidden acts of kindness and wisdom that keep their loved ones and the community on the right path.

Through Rachel's efforts, Akiva eventually became a scholar who enabled Judaism to survive anywhere, even under tyranny. The Judaism that he taught and developed provided a treasure, from which "new treasures might be continually extracted," and through which they could draw closer together.[3] He codified what was to be

---

[3] Ginzberg, Louis. *Akiba ben Joseph*, at www.jewishencyclopedia.com.

the Jewish Bible and its "unchangeableness," and he provided a way for Jews to develop Judaism through creative interpretation of every or any of its letters and words, "to discover things that were even unknown to Moses."[4] This system of interpretation was known as the Oral Law, which continues to evolve according to Akiva's methods.

As a shepherd, Akiva was bitter and blamed Jewish leadership for the destruction of their state. What transformed Akiva from an illiterate laborer into a leader who gave the Jewish world its spiritual lifeline? What did Rachel see in him, and what was her part in his transformation? Here is her story.

Q: WELCOME, Rachel.

Rachel: Thank you. I understand you have the State of Israel as a Jewish homeland again. I am so happy to hear that! When I lived, Jerusalem was in ruins and most of the Jews who could escape had fled to other countries. Families were torn apart, often for good. Those of us who stayed suffered under Roman rule. Life was difficult.

Q: How did Jews keep their faith alive during this time?

Rachel: It was hard. Without the Temple, the debates of Jewish law and how to practice it were fierce. What to do was discussed in and out of the courts, in every home and at the table of every scholar of the time.

Q: It sounds like there was quite a lot of confusion.

Rachel: Yes, there was. Jewish leaders struggled for answers to people's dilemmas of how to comply with Roman laws when the alternative was death.

Q: Tell us your story.

Rachel: During my time, Jewish history was already rich in tradition. We were terribly concerned that it would disappear. Jews

---

[4] Ibid.

had become a nation before they had a land. We could survive without a land once again if we had to, but how could we keep our tradition and law alive while we were so scattered and oppressed?

Q: What was your family like? Where did you live?

Rachel: Although I did not come from a family of scholars, I had a comfortable upbringing in Jerusalem. My father was Kalba Savua, a wealthy businessman. His wealth and status bought safety and leniency for our family and our close associates and workers. We were among the lucky few who had survived the Roman siege.

My father insisted that I study Jewish history and traditions and arranged for private tutors for me. Learning came easily to me, and I had a natural and instinctive appreciation for the decisions and discussions of the rabbis. I had great respect for the intellectual depth of our leaders and their efforts to keep Judaism a viable religion.

Q: Were you ever tempted to leave Judaism because of the pressure of the Roman occupation?

Rachel: No. Giving up or marrying outside of Judaism was not an option in my family. I had many suitors as a young woman. My father would have been happy to see me marry any one of them, but I was interested only in Akiva, one of the shepherds who worked for my father. Whenever I went out to read or study, sitting under a tree overlooking the hills, I always saw him. He would look at me and then avert his eyes, and stare curiously at my books. One day when our eyes met, I decided to approach him. I wanted to speak to him, so as he turned to run, I motioned him to stay. He was shy and seemed almost too humble to engage in conversation with someone with books.

Q: There were books then?

Rachel: We did, but not the way you do today. Our books were scrolls written on parchment, much like the Torah scroll that we read from.

One day, when Akiva and I began to talk, I noticed something about him that the sages later discovered; although he was "unassuming, there was something extraordinary about him."[5] After many weeks of meeting and talking, he confided to me that he was a Jew, living under the protection of my father, Kalba Savua. His family had fled Israel but he had wanted to stay. He was living in the fields alone, avoiding the attention of the occupiers.[6] He had no education and knew little of our history and traditions, having been left to survive on his own as a child.

Q: What was so extraordinary about him?

Rachel: He was curious and interested in the Jewish people. He would often venture into the marketplace where, risking his life, he absorbed what was happening in Jerusalem. He became intensely interested in everything I was learning. When I shared the content of my lessons with him, he grasped their essence effortlessly. What was also extraordinary was that after I described some of the recent decisions and rulings of the rabbis, he had strong opinions. He found those decisions too rigid, since he believed that Judaism should be a religion of love, compassion and optimism for the future. He felt the leaders should be giving people better tools to get through these times of uncertainty.[7]

His own ideas of how to interpret the Torah appealed to me. One day, he told me, "If the rabbis were so wise, they could have prevented the destruction of our Temple." I was shocked but could not help agreeing with him. The Temple indeed had been corrupted by the immoral conduct of the priesthood and their desecration of the values that it represented.

Q: It sounds as if he was more than a simple shepherd.

Rachel: He was so much more. He was deeply involved in his Judaism and quite passionate about it. His anger and resentment only showed that he felt he could do a better job than the current

---

[5] *The Book of Legends,* 233.

[6] His full name was Akiva ben Joseph. See the entry at www.jewishencyclopedia.com.

[7] Rabbi Bill Berk of the Shalom Hartman Institute on the fragility of life and optimism of Judaism. Shalom Hartman Institute online.

leadership. He saw many ways to turn tragedy into lessons for life, and to allow Judaism to evolve into a positive personal experience, something we needed badly at the time. I knew that if only he had the opportunity to learn and study, he could grow to be a valuable force in Jewish life and a great leader.

Q: Did anyone notice that you were getting involved with him?

Rachel: I don't know. I was too absorbed in thinking of him all the time, drawn in by his charisma. We were two like-minded young people and as we talked more and more, I enjoyed his sharp and brilliant mind. To me it seemed a waste that he worked as a shepherd when he could do so much more. Our community needed him. I needed him. And I began to love him.

Q: Were you afraid that you might regret your love for Akiva one day?

Rachel: No. I loved Akiva and believed in him, and nothing else mattered. As we sat in the valley behind my family's estate, I knew we belonged together. Our love for each other blossomed and we talked of marriage. But it was not easy. Our engagement became the first test of our love.

Q: Your family didn't want you to marry an illiterate shepherd.

Rachel: Of course not. But there was another challenge. I believed so much in Akiva's potential that I insisted that he give up his disdain for the rabbis and enter their academies to study. We as Jews had all heard the voice at Sinai. Now Akiva would have to hear that voice discussed, argued, and explained in the academies of learning. Only there could he develop his thoughts, and it was there that his ideas would make a difference to our people.

Q: How did he react to your directing his life in this way?

Rachel: He showed tremendous relief that finally, someone had recognized his inner world.

Q: Why would he have to learn Hebrew? What language did you speak if not Hebrew?

Rachel: We used Hebrew for prayer, but Aramaic was our everyday language then.

Q: Why Aramaic?

Rachel: The first time that Israel was destroyed and lost its sovereignty,[8] Jews settled in lands where Aramaic was the common language of the people. Aramaic was spoken from the Mediterranean Sea to the Euphrates River, and it was adopted by the Jews living in these areas. Israel's foreign occupiers also spoke it, so even the Jews who stayed adopted Aramaic as their everyday language. Hebrew was used in the academies and in the circles of the learned. Aramaic remained the popular language even when the Jews returned to Israel, up to our day.

When the rabbis began writing the Talmud, the Mishnah, our oral laws, were written in Hebrew. Yet the Gemara – the intricate discussions and debates of those laws – was written in Aramaic, recorded as they were spoken.

Q: Let's go back to you and Akiva. You became engaged. And then?

Rachel: It was hard to break the news to my family. They were mortified.

Q: They had no sympathy for your love?

Rachel: None at all. No one cared about my love for Akiva or heard my pleas for understanding. My father, who was furious that I had flouted his authority, banished me from the only home I had ever known. He disowned and disinherited me by a formal vow. Yet even though this caused me terrible pain, or perhaps because it did, I clung to Akiva and my vision for him with greater determination.

Q: What did you do?

---

[8] In 586 B.C.E.; see above.

Rachel: Akiva and I left my father's estate and lived as paupers. We found shelter in fields and were dependent on the mercy of kind farmers. Since we both loved nature and each other, our existence in the fields was an adventure. We discovered the miracles of our land, hidden natural springs and small quiet streams that fed fruits and flowers. Akiva and I were so much in love that we hardly noticed our hardship. We slept on straw in the barns and stables of merciful land-owners. In the morning, Akiva would pick straw from my hair and say, "If I had the means, I would give you a gold tiara with the word 'Jerusalem' engraved on it."[9]

We were young, idealistic, and undeterred by the occupiers who ravaged the country. But we were also wise enough to stay far from their reach and lucky not to be discovered.

Q: Since you both respected Jewish tradition, how could you live together without being married?

Rachel: The first thing we did was to sneak into Jerusalem one night and find an old family friend of mine who was now a rabbi serving a small school and prayer hall. He was protected by wealthy patrons who had bribed the local Roman officials to ignore its existence. This rabbi married us in a simple ceremony. I won't describe my dress, except to say that it had been a favorite of mine that I had only worn on special occasions and snatched from my closet when I left home. I had kept it rolled up in my bundle all this time, but miraculously it was clean enough for me to wear for the ceremony.

Q: It sounds like quite an adventure.

Rachel: It was only the beginning. We lived from hand to mouth, and before long, I gave birth to our first son. The same rabbi who married us circumcised him, and we named him Simeon. We couldn't have been happier. Soon afterwards, I gave birth to another son, Joshua. We were blissfully busy, but I had not forgotten Akiva's promise to go to an academy to sharpen his

---

[9] *The Book of Legends*, 233, #145.

brilliant mind. I still believed he could be the leader that the Jewish people desperately needed in these times of tyranny and transition.

Q: You were prepared to let him go, leaving you in such difficult circumstances?

Rachel: There was no choice but to let him go. How else would he fulfill his destiny? He certainly was not going to accomplish much as a wandering pauper!

Q: You are yet another great woman who stands behind a great man. What would Akiva have been without you?

Rachel: I don't usually answer hypothetical questions, but here's an answer. It's not enough just to dream. We also have to make our dreams happen.

By the time Akiva left to study, we had added two girls to our family. Caring for the children was my best comfort and distraction. Despite my wanting to be by Akiva's side all the time, I pushed him out the door to begin his journey. Little did I know that the future of the Jewish world depended on that push. When he left, we were drenched in tears, but we were also excited about the future.

Q: You showed such foresight that you could qualify as a prophet.

Rachel: I don't think so. I think it was intuition and the fact that I was strong and stubborn. I prayed for the day when Akiva would return as the hero that I believed he could be.

Q: Did Akiva know where he was going?

Rachel: Yes. He chose a small rural school where he could learn Hebrew. This was the first step because the Torah was written in Hebrew.

He was not embarrassed to study with six-year-old boys. The teachers were awed by Akiva's enthusiasm and capacity to learn quickly. When he began to study Torah, they noticed his extraordinary ability to retain its content, together with the lessons of the sages. Eventually, they recommended that he attend a more advanced school: the academy of the most learned rabbis, Eliezer and Yehoshua.

Q: How long was Akiva away?

Rachel: At first, he was away for twelve years. After all that time, his hunger for learning was still insatiable. He relentlessly plied Rabbi Eliezer and Rabbi Yehoshua with questions until they admitted that they were out of answers. They gave him high praise, affirming that he was producing his own brilliant arguments in Jewish law and insights in Torah. They told Akiva that he was ready to leave their academy and become a teacher in his own right. By then, he had his own following of students who absorbed his every word. This was the beginning of the fulfillment of our dream.

Q: How did you survive, raising children alone, with little means?

Rachel: The reports I heard of Akiva's success and the reputation he was building made me happy. I sold what I could – pieces of embroidered cloth and bundles of wood. I worked for food, and when our sons were old enough, they joined their father. My friends, who were as poor as we were, couldn't understand my steady optimism.

Q: Had Akiva become a rabbi by then?

Rachel: Yes. He had his own academy, with many students. His return home was magnificent.

Q: What happened? What was it like?

Rachel: Before Akiva arrived, my friends wanted me to put on a dress that was not torn, since by now, even my wedding dress was in shreds. I didn't care. I was so confident that our reunion would be glorious no matter what I wore that I quoted to them from Proverbs: "A righteous man will recognize his loyal creature."[10]

My friends thought that I was out of my mind. When Akiva appeared in the neighborhood square, his students saw me running towards him and tried to protect him from what they thought was a pauper grabbing him in the fervor of the moment. He recognized me immediately and stopped them, telling them all with great

---

[10] Proverbs 12:10; *The Book of Legends*, 233, #145.

humility and grace: "Let her be! What is mine and yours are rightly hers."[11]

Q: He gave you all the credit.

Rachel: It was a highly emotional moment. All my dreams for him had come true. I don't know how many students he had, but according to legend, the number reached twenty-four thousand.

Q: What about your father? Now that Akiva was not only learned but also well known, did he continue to reject you? Were you still estranged from your family?

Rachel: Apparently, even though my father now regretted having made the vow by which he disowned and disinherited me, he could not break it because vows were taken very seriously then. However, a vow could be annulled in the presence of a rabbi and witnesses. When my father heard that a great rabbi had come to Jerusalem, he said, "I shall go to him. Perhaps the great man will release me from my vow."

Q: What happened when they met?

Rachel: The Talmud tells us:

> When the father came to him, Rabbi Akiva asked, "Would you have made your vow if you had known that [your daughter's] husband was to become a great man?" The father replied, "[Had her husband known] even one chapter, even one halachah, [I would not have made such a vow.]" Rabbi Akiva then said, "I am your daughter's husband." The father fell upon his face and kissed Rabbi Akiva's feet. Presently, he gave him half of his wealth.[12]

Q: So now, after so many years of poverty, you were wealthy and on good terms with your father once more. How did your lives change?

---

[11] *The Book of Legends,* 233, #145.
[12] *The Book of Legends,* 233, #145.

Rachel: The first thing Akiva did was to fulfill an old promise that he had made to me when we were first married. He bought me a beautiful gold tiara, part of customary formal wear. It was engraved with the word "Jerusalem" and set with precious stones.

He established a new academy and we also used our resources to help the poor. It was a happy time. Some say that I had the most power of anyone because I had vision of what would be good for me, for my husband, and our people.[13]

Q: Did you feel powerful?

Rachel: In some ways, yes. But the credit goes to Rabbi Akiva. He did great things such as helping codify what would become the Tanach, the Bible, known as the Written Torah. So sensitive was he to the entirety of the Jewish people that he insisted on including the Song of Songs, a highly erotic, sensual poem because he recognized that every Jew should experience the profound emotion of a loving relationship. To him, this poem was a paradigm for the love between the Jewish people and God. Most of the other rabbis protested his insistence that it be included in the canon, but my husband prevailed.

He insisted that the Book of Esther be included as well because, as he saw it, Esther's story shows how Jews can control their own destiny. As he saw it, Esther's story demonstrates how each one of us is responsible for Judaism's survival even when God appears to be hidden, and that even then, we are still full partners with the Divine! Although there was controversy about including the Book of Esther, the rabbis finally agreed with Rabbi Akiva. Not only that – they also taught that in the Messianic Era, no holidays will be celebrated except for Purim because on Purim, we willingly took responsibility for our relationship with God.

Q: What else is Akiva known for?

---

[13] Abrams, Judith Z. *The Women of the Talmud.* New York: Jason Aronson, Rowman & Littlefield, 1992, 67–68.

Rachel: He taught that as we no longer had the Temple, our relationship with God must become more personal. Each and every Jew could now undertake the practices of atonement, prayer and service to God without the priests acting as intermediaries. The daily sacrifices would be replaced by daily prayer. He taught that without a Temple, the distance between God and Jew was indeed smaller – a good thing, even if it came out of sad circumstances.

Q: Many centuries later, the Chief Rabbi of the United Kingdom wrote that because of Rabbi Akiva, there was now egalitarian spirituality, in which every Jew is holy and personal prayer brings us closer, and atonement for wrongdoing is accomplished by personal repentance and changing our behavior.[14]

Rachel: How wonderful that a leader of your generation understands and approves of my husband's actions!

Q: Your husband was also known for his optimism. Can you give us an example?

Rachel: Yes. Once, while Akiva was walking with several of his colleagues, they saw a fox emerging from the place where the Holy of Holies had been. His colleagues began to weep. Do you know what Akiva did? He laughed! When his scandalized colleagues asked him how he could laugh at such a dreadful sight, he explained: just as the prophecy that foxes would inhabit the Holy of Holies had come true, the prophecies that the Temple would be rebuilt would also come true. He also created the partner method of Torah study, which is still known by its ancient name, *havruta* – "friend."

Q: It sounds as if life maintained some semblance of normality despite the Roman occupation. How did it affect you?

Rachel: It was a constant threat, actually. My husband was often drawn into the public debates that the Romans used in order to mock us. When they discovered that Akiva was a supporter of

---

[14] Sacks, Rabbi Jonathan. *A Letter in the Scroll*. New York: The Free Press, 2000, 148–150.

124

Bar Kochba, who led an uprising against them, they threw him into prison. He continued to teach by word of mouth even from his cell. Even in prison, Akiva was still a pillar of hope and courage to his fellow Jews.

Q: What happened then?

Rachel: The Talmud recounts how the Romans sentenced Akiva to death, and tore his flesh from his body with iron combs. But he hardly felt any pain at all. Even his executioners, amazed at his courage, asked him whether he was a sorcerer. He answered that he was no such thing, that he was grateful for the opportunity to show his love for his Creator to the very last moment of his life. And then he died, affirming God's oneness with his last breath.

Q: Do you wonder about the justice of your husband's death?

Rachel: You are the justice. You are alive and thriving as Jews in spite of the many cruel powers that have risen to destroy us. They have vanished, but we live on. Judaism is a religion of love and optimism because of the tools that Rabbi Akiva gave us to use every day to mend the world.

Q: It's not easy for young people to remain committed Jews in the modern world.

Rachel: Nor was it for us. My husband believed in a personal Judaism that one can experience under any circumstances. Also, today you have the State of Israel. When is it ever easy? But it is possible.

Q: Thank you, Rachel.

RACHEL, JOCHEVED, AND MIRIAM

THE DAUGHTERS OF RASHI

WHO WAS RASHI, who were his daughters and how do they fit into a book about Jewish heroes?

Rabbi Shlomo Yitzhaki (1040–1105)[1], who is better known by the acronym Rashi, lived in Troyes, France, with his wife and three daughters, Rachel, Jocheved, and Miriam.

How did Jews reach Europe in general, and in France in particular?

Jews lived in Europe as far back as the Roman conquest of Israel at the beginning of the Common Era. Many were taken to Rome as slaves, and upon gaining their freedom, chose to stay in Rome. Others migrated for other reasons, so that by 200 C.E., there were more than one hundred thousand Jews living in Rome. Then, as the Romans conquered France and Germany, Jews followed and established the first Jewish communities in Central Europe. By 300 C.E., there were Jewish communities in Paris, Lyons, and cities along the Rhine such as Treves, Cologne, and Mayence. They were welcomed because they reputedly improved the economy wherever they went. In 1084, the Bishop of Speyer by the Rhine wrote: "Desiring to make a town out of the village of Speyer, I thought to raise its dignity many times by getting Jews to settle there." The Emperor Charlemagne, founder of the Holy Roman Empire, and his son Louis, protected Jews from Church oppression because "…Jews became so important in the economic life of the medieval

---

[1] Apparently, he often signed his name in this way. *Rashi: Commentaries on the Pentateuch.* Selected and Translated by Chaim Pearl. New York: W.W. Norton & Company, 1970, 15.

community that the market day was changed from Saturday to Sunday (or sometimes a weekday). Although Jews could not own land in many parts of Europe in the Middle Ages, in this early period, Jews did own and farm land, particularly in France."[2]

Rashi was a modern rabbi for the Middle Ages, since he was at ease with both Jewish and Christian leaders and neighbors. He believed in the universality of faith, kindness and peace. A businessman as well as a great scholar, his greatest contribution to Judaism and the world was that he simplified the meaning of the Talmud. His clear and succinct interpretations made it more accessible to everyone as a valuable source of civil and religious law. While Maimonides "is regarded as medieval Judaism's greatest philosopher and intellect, Rashi is its greatest teacher.... Had Rashi not written a Talmud commentary that explained its difficult Aramaic words and guided students through its intricate and often confusing forms of logic, the Talmud might have become a largely forgotten work."[3]

Rashi's daughters were favored students and by the end of his life, they themselves were so learned and accomplished in Jewish law and custom that they wrote answers to questions of Jewish law on their father's behalf. They are models of the ability to pursue one's passion and break through social bias to fulfill a destiny one believes in.

Rachel speaks to us on behalf of her older sisters, Jocheved and Miriam.

Q: WELCOME, Rachel. We in modern times have a picture of Medieval Europe as a dark and fearful place for Jews. Is this the way life was?

Rachel: The common belief that Jewish life in medieval Europe "was an unbroken story of persecution is not quite

---

[2] Pearl, 12.
[3] *Jewish Literacy,* 180.

accurate."[4] Although we felt insecure and knew that we were often welcomed into a community only because we were good for the economy, we still lived freely as Jews. We were great travelers and merchants, bringing goods from the East to Europe.[5] In this way, we kept strong ties to other Jewish communities, all of whom were also involved in trade. This enhanced and expanded our own commercial enterprises – and naturally benefited our host countries. We were a good source of taxation for king and lord alike, bolstering the local governments in which we lived. For these reasons, the local rulers protected us from anti-Semitic dictates of the Church in Rome.

Q: Does this era compare to the flourishing of Jewish life in Spain?

Rachel: Yes – but there, the Jews lived under Muslim rule. While Spain became the focal point for the study and elucidation of Jewish religious philosophy and the home of Hebrew poetry, Germany and France were regarded as the major locales for Talmud and Bible study.[6] My father was the son of a scholar in France, where the center of Jewish cultural activity was in the south, in Provence, and students of Talmud came from all over Europe to study in its academies. Rabbis came from Italy, which had served as the bridge for the transference of knowledge from the Talmudic academies of Babylon.[7]

Q: Tell us more about the France you grew up in.

Rachel: My father was born in 1040 in Troyes, which was the chief city of the Duchy of Champagne, one of the most important of the twelve duchies or counties (of France). The city, which was situated on an important route to the North and held biennial trade fairs, was a large trading center. When I was born, about one hundred Jewish families lived in Troyes, and they were active in

---

[4] Pearl, 11.

[5] Ibid.

[6] Pearl, 12–13.

[7] Ibid.

every branch of trade. Some families, like my own, owned and cultivated vineyards, employed local laborers and produced the sparkling wine for which the district became famous – champagne![8]

Q: It sounds like life was good. How did you get along with your Christian neighbors?

Rachel: We lived next to each other, in the same neighborhoods, and spoke their native language, French. We even gave them "gifts on Purim… and often they brought food to [us] on the last day of Passover… [so that we could] eat unleavened food at the end of the festival."[9]

Q: Tell us about your father.

Rachel: My father was an erudite man, but along with his strong gifts for learning and scholarship, he was also a maker of fine champagne. When he was old enough to leave his parents, he traveled to Talmudic academies in Mayence and Worms to satisfy his thirst for knowledge. He studied and taught there, and later moved to Worms on the Rhine.

Q: There is a small chapel in Worms, "the legendary seat at which Rashi taught."[10] It was destroyed by the Nazis but rebuilt after World War II as a tribute to him. People visit it in homage and reverence to your father.

Rachel: He would be humbled to know this.

When he was twenty-five, he returned to Troyes with a small following of students and founded his own academy. Its reputation later rivaled all others in Europe and it is here that he started writing his Commentaries on the Bible and the Talmud. While pursuing his religious and intellectual work, he was active in business in Champagne, as well as the social life of our

---

[8] Ibid, 13.
[9] Pearl, 13.
[10]Pearl, 16.

community.[11] He refused to take a salary as a teacher, choosing instead to earn a living from his vineyards. The whole family went into the fields when the grapes were ready for gathering.

Q: Tell us about daily life in your household.

Rachel: Our house was constantly full of activity because we hosted many students who studied at my father's academy. Our table was covered either with hearty meals or with cakes, sweets and tea. For my sisters and myself, times were interesting. The finest young men of Europe would come to our table, where lively debates and conversations animated each meal and afterwards, when my father's students returned to the academy, my sisters and I loved to talk about the men – which was the most talented, the handsomest, or had the most personality. We didn't hesitate to offer our opinions to my father, who delighted in our participation.

By the time we were ten years old, my father had taught us to read and write Hebrew. We studied with him privately every evening after his long hours in the vineyards or teaching. As soon as he walked through the front door, we pulled our chairs to the dining table where paper, pen, and ink had been set out after the last meal of the day, waiting for us to gather around. It was my favorite time of day. It was so peaceful. My mother rested from her busy day, and we listened to my father teach. When we were old enough to understand, he shaped every word of Torah into a *drash*, a story told from the essence of its meaning. What I remember best is his warm smile of deep satisfaction when we asked him questions, trying to equal his wisdom. He delighted in our attempts to surpass him. It usually fell to me to record what we had learned, and gradually I took on the role as my father's assistant as he wrote answers to halachic questions, called *responsa*, to many people who sought his advice on how to live and practice a Jewish life.

Q: What about the debate over girls studying Torah and Talmud in those days? That controversy has lasted until today. I am sure you

---

[11] Ibid, 16–17.

remember that according to the Talmud, a man may teach his daughter Greek "because knowledge of the language is deemed an accomplishment."[12] In the case of learning Torah, some have written that women should only be taught the essentials in order to pass them on to her children, but not the meanings and specific details, since they cannot understand them as well as men can.[13]

And then there is the opinion in the Babylonian Talmud, Tractate *Sotah* 20a, which some rabbis have interpreted as a prohibition against women studying Torah. It reads as follows: "Declared Ben Azzai: 'A man must teach his daughter Torah so that if she drinks [the bitter water of the *sotah* ordeal], she will know that her merit will suspend her punishment. But Rav Eliezer said, "Whoever teaches his daughter Torah teaches her *tiflut*" (nonsense).[14]

What is your analysis of this text? Considering how commonly it was adopted, how did your father manage to teach his daughters Torah and Talmud while keeping his reputation intact?

Rachel: In our day, it was common that girls from scholarly families learn Hebrew and Torah. After all, Jewish education was the family business. In addition, Judaism always accepts exceptions on individual bases. There is a long history of learned and scholarly Jewish women.

Often, women and young girls did not have time to pursue studies since they had all the responsibilities of the household. Remember that back then, there were no modern conveniences. The rabbis felt that women should not be distracted by the burdens of learning Torah. While boys and men had more obligations in everyday observance, all children, boys *and* girls learned the basics of Torah in order to live a life accordingly. My father was exceptional in his encouraging anyone to learn. He would have thought it blasphemous to discourage us from learning, and he

---

[12] JT *Shabbat* 6:1, 7d. *The Book of Legends*, 290, #476.

[13] *Midrash Rabbah* 28:2, Exodus. *The Book of Legends*, 80, #37.

[14] Mishnah *Sotah* 3:4. *Jewish Women in Historical Perspective*, 81.

never feared what others might think as he raised us to be scholars. We even wore *tefillin* when we prayed.[15] Our father encouraged us in all of the ways that one can grow closer to God.

Finally, all these opinions in the Talmud show how Judaism is open to many opinions, and that our learning is an exercise in democracy and freedom. While some rabbis expressed these opinions, they were not necessarily accepted as law or custom.

Q: But how did your father explain his teaching women if anyone mentioned this Talmudic source?

Rachel: He referred to the *Midrash*.[16] Deuteronomy 6:7 says, regarding God's commandments, "You shall teach them diligently *li-vanecha* – your sons." The Midrash explains that the word "sons" actually refers to disciples, thus removing gender distinction from the Hebrew word. If males and females are referred to together, the Hebrew uses only the masculine plural to include both genders. My father felt no gender distinctions in the pursuit of Torah knowledge.[17]

Q: Although your father's well-known commentary on the Talmud was left incomplete, it was continued by his grandson Samuel. However, there are responsa whose authorship is in doubt, and it is believed that you or your sisters wrote them.

Rachel: We did. Towards the end of his life, my father would discuss the possible answers to questions that people were asking while I acted as his secretary.[18] I continued his work after he died,

---

[15] *Jewish Literacy,* 661–662. "Tefillin are biblical in origin…. They are two small black boxes with black straps attached to them; Jewish men are required to place one box on their head and tie the other one on their arm each weekday morning…. The text that is inserted inside the two boxes of tefillin is hand-written by a scribe and consists of the four sets of biblical verses in which tefillin are commanded (Exodus 13:1–10, 11–16; Deuteronomy 6:4–9, 11:13–21)."

[16] *Jewish Literacy,* 156–158. "Midrash most commonly refers to… a compilation of the rabbis' comments on each of the five volumes of the Torah."

[17] Sifre, Deuteronomy, #34. *The Book of Legends,* 415, #125.

[18] Baskin, 126, n. 66.

helping people in their quest to live according to Jewish custom and law. No one seemed to notice that the responsa were mine. For example, there was a controversy at the time as to whether a woman may recite the blessing over the Sabbath lights. Until then, men had done so. This question was resolved by my niece, who wrote a responsum that explained how my sister always performed the ritual at home. From then on, the issue seemed to be settled.[19]

Q: And thus it is today.

I have a question, however. Why was your father so troubled about Beruria?

Rachel: Do you mean Beruria from the Talmud? Please refresh my memory.

Q: Yes. The Talmud mentions Beruria as a scholar. It quotes her many times, more than it quotes any other woman, and notes that she was well versed in both the Written and Oral Law.

Rachel: The Talmud also records that Beruria never hesitated to speak her mind, sometimes rather sharply.

Q: Yes, that is true. Could that be the reason why your father evidently wrote, or perhaps merely quoted, a midrash in which Beruria comes to a sad and sordid end? According to this story, her husband Rabbi Meir, who apparently wanted to take her down a peg, put one of his students up to seducing her. Beruria refused at first, but eventually the student wore down her resistance, and she accepted his invitation. When she realized what she had agreed to, she ended her life out of shame.

Can this story possibly be true? Surely your father would never use Beruria to support the cliché that women who deviate from accepted custom come to a bad end. There is no evidence to support this story. Can you explain why your father wrote about Beruria as he did?

---

[19] Anton, Maggie. *Rashi's Daughters, Book I: Joheved.* New York: A Plume Book, 2007, 354.

Rachel: Some say that he "felt the need to discredit Beruriah to prove his loyalty to patriarchal tradition, since [we], like Beruria, studied Torah and wore *tefillin,* which was considered bold and scandalous behavior in [the] Orthodox community."[20] While he may have felt some peer pressure, he never shared this midrash with us. To quote some of my father's written commentaries on particular verses in Tanach, "I do not understand it."

Q: I have asked many rabbis in my own day. None of them feels that this account is compatible with his respect for women's intellect. It is no wonder that scholars of Rashi often begin with the question: "What was troubling Rashi?"

Rachel: In over seventy cases, my father admitted that he could not understand a particular point.[21]

Q: What was he most famous for?

Rachel: My father was a master at simplifying and "revitalizing the sacred texts and explain[ing] the meaning of the Talmud."[22] He is renowned among scholars for the clear and simple style of his commentary because his objective was always "to explain the text as it stands…. The single question Rashi answered is: What does the particular word or phrase signify? He was most interested in plain meaning and then its "implied ethical teaching." But the plain and simple meaning always had to support any such interpretation.[23] Then he would include his own thoughts, drawing ideas from his encyclopedic knowledge of all aspects of Torah.

In his Talmud commentary, he doesn't explain the sages' discussions, but rather offers "meaning to the word or phrase which needs explanation in order to help the reader understand the text. What [we] find… is really what the Talmud text itself says. This is the clue to Rashi's entire method."

---

[20] Frankel, Ellen. *The Five Books of Miriam.* San Francisco: Harper, 1996, 313.

[21] Pearl, 22–23.

[22] Ibid, 16.

[23] Ibid, 19.

Q: The challenge of simplicity is great.

Rachel: Without my father's commentaries, I am sure the Talmud would "have remained a totally neglected book except for the experts and a small group of scholars. With Rashi, Talmud study remained alive for the people."[24]

Q: What was your father like as a person?

Rachel: He was popular and sociable with everyone. As a rabbi, he inclined towards leniency and compassion in his advice. When Jews who had converted to Christianity under duress wanted to return to Judaism after the oppression had lifted, he advocated welcoming them back in the easiest way. He was quietly pious, kind to all, and loved and respected by both Jews and non-Jews. He even attracted a Christian monk who heard about him and wanted to study with him. This monk later influenced theologians such as Martin Luther in their method of translating Bible in the simplest manner.

Q: I learned something about your father that is an example of his far-reaching influence in the world. Apparently, the image of an angel as a child with wings was his idea. When Protestant scholars asked him what he thought the cherubim in the bible looked like, he answered, "A young child with wings." Since that time, religion, art, and literature have portrayed them in that manner.[25]

Rachel: I remember him discussing how he wanted to answer in a way that they could easily relate to the image. During that moment, I felt that the Divine Presence had embraced all our communities.

Q: It is a testimony to your father that the very first Hebrew book to be printed on a printing press – in Reggio, Italy, in 1475 – was his commentary on the Pentateuch. Then, in 1482, the Torah with

---

[24] Pearl, 27.

[25] From the weekly class on the Torah portion, Parashat Terumah, given by Rabbi Chaim Steinmetz. Montreal, February 2008.

your father's commentary in the margin was printed in Bologna, Italy.[26] You must be so proud!

Can you explain what "Rashi script" is? His commentary is written in the margins of many texts in what seems to look like a different alphabet.

Rachel: It is a cursive script that was chosen by the printer. The first edition of Rashi, which was printed in 1475, appeared in this printing font, which became known afterwards as "Rashi script." Of a different appearance from the square Assyrian script, it was used presumably because the letters are smaller and allow greater economy in writing material.[27] But my father never wrote this way.

Q: In 1095, Jews in the nearby Rhineland suffered in the First Crusade, which was called by Pope Urban II in Rome. Jews were murdered and their homes destroyed. This must have been devastating. Did you sense the tide was turning for Jews of Europe?

Rachel: Since I was twenty-six years old when it happened, I remember it well. My life was shattered when some of our family who lived along the Rhine became victims of the massacre. My father, who had always been hopeful and positive about life, became sad and bitter. He began to write *selihot,* penitential prayers that expressed his mood. Although local lords and dukes often protected us, it was not they who increasingly withdrew our rights and dignity. The evil decrees emanated from Rome, where the papacy blamed Jews for everything from disease and natural phenomena to the Protestant Reformation. This was how Europe entered the Middle Ages.

Since most of our family was spared, we were able to keep my father's legacy alive. My brothers-in-law and great-nephews became well-known rabbis whose commentaries also surround the text of the Talmud. They developed my father's teaching system further

---

[26] Pearl, 23.

[27] Werblowsky and Wigoder. *Encyclopedia of the Jewish Religion.* New York: Holt, Rinehart, and Winston Inc., 1965, 322.

and tried to answer the questions that he couldn't. The women in our family remained examples in the intellectual and spiritual realms.

Q: What would you tell those who feel that religion has no meaning for them today, that the commandments are irrelevant and of no consequence in modern life? On the one hand, there are many creative efforts to re-interpret Judaism to make it more meaningful and egalitarian. There is even a renaissance in Jewish learning, particularly among women. But at the same time, religion has never been so challenged. Books and films that preach its irrelevance are popular all over the world.

Rachel: I would say: Stay with it and struggle with it, be creative, but don't ever abandon it. It is relevant, especially in challenging times. Re-interpret it with respect for the past and optimism for the future, but don't leave it. Wrestle with it and unfold it more, so that it speaks to your generation. Create positive and engaging experiences that speak to people's emotions and senses, and that highlight the joy and optimism of Judaism. If we continue to learn what it is that God wants from His world,[28] we will live forever.

Q: Thank you, Rachel.

---

[28] Steinsaltz, Adin. *Opening the Tanya.* San Francisco: Jossey-Bass, 2003, 146.

Dona Gracia Nasi

ALMOST TWO THOUSAND YEARS after the Book of Esther's story, there lived a woman named Dona Gracia Nasi, for whom Esther was a role model. Like Esther, Gracia Nasi helped her fellow Jews during a period in history when they were targeted, this time by the Catholic Church in Rome.

Gracia Nasi's story takes place in the 1500s C.E. The persecution that marked her era was the Spanish Inquisition.[1] Gracia Nasi used her family's wealth to emerge from a comfortable life and become a hero, saving many Jewish lives. Like Esther, she hid her Jewish identity as she grew up in luxurious surroundings. Her brother was the personal physician to the King of Portugal.

Historically, both Gracia and Esther came from the line of Jewish royalty that dates back to ancient Israel. Gracia Nasi could trace her lineage to King David, while Esther could trace hers to King Saul. Perhaps both women were related in the way their lives unfolded, as well as by blood. Esther paved the way for a Jewish return to Israel and the rebuilding of the Second Temple that re-established Jewish kingship. Gracia Nasi paved a route for persecuted Jews of Western Europe to reach religious freedom in Israel and rekindled the spark to re-establish sovereignty there.

How did Jews like Gracia Nasi and her family come to live in Western Europe?

When the Second Temple in Jerusalem was destroyed in 70 C.E., Jews were exiled just as they had been in 586 B.C.E., when the First Temple was destroyed. In this second exile, the largest community settled in the countries north, east and south of Israel, where they were allowed to form societies with their own leadership and court of law. The leader, who was called the Nasi (prince; plural *Nesi'im*),

---

[1] *Jewish Literacy*, 190–192.

served as both the political and scholarly leader of the Sanhedrin. The *Nesi'im*, who were chosen because they were believed to be direct descendants of King David, were an "ancient and memorable clan" who gradually dispersed across North Africa and eventually reached the Iberian Peninsula. By the twelfth century, Jewish life in Spain was thriving. Rabbis and scholars studied, taught and wrote prolifically, and many of their writings are studied to this very day. These were Gracia Nasi's roots.[2]

But the Jews felt the impending threat as early as the beginning of the fourteenth century, when official persecutions began. These intensified with the massacre of 1391 and culminated in the Edict of Expulsion in 1492, when Queen Isabella, wishing to make Spain a purely Catholic country, decreed that all Jews must leave Spanish soil. Gracia Nasi's family, like thousands of others, fled to Portugal where they were accepted by the Portuguese government, more as a measure to benefit the economy than as an act of kindness toward this proud and persecuted people. Her family, which was wealthy, could afford to pay the special tax that allowed them to live in a respectable neighborhood of Lisbon.

However, in time, all the Jews of Portugal had to pay a much higher price to ensure their safety: they had to renounce their Judaism. They lived outwardly as Christians while maintaining Jewish tradition secretly in their homes. They attended church, participated in Christian rituals and life cycle events, and were even buried in Christian cemeteries. These secret Jews, or "New Christians," were called *conversos* (converts), but in Spain and Portugal they were called *marrano*s, meaning "swine" in Spanish.

Yet even the public conversion of the Jews of Portugal was not enough to save them from bloodshed. Riots continued in Lisbon against *conversos,* and many were killed. When the King of Portugal, bowing to increasing pressure from the Pope in Rome, tried to introduce the Inquisition into his country, wealthy *converso* families,

---

[2] Roth, Cecil. *Dona Gracia of the House of Nasi.* Philadelphia: JPS, 1948, chapter 1.

like Gracia's, paid the king large ransoms to postpone the act. Jewish life was tenuous at best.

Q: DONA GRACIA NASI, please tell us about yourself.

Gracia Nasi: I was born in Lisbon in 1510 into a wealthy *converso* family. Although my mother died when my sister and I were very young, our family was close and we were nurtured by relatives and guardians who were also *conversos*, loving and grateful for the safety and protection.

Q: You remind us of Queen Esther of Persia, who also lost her mother at a young age.

Gracia Nasi: Once I knew that I was Jewish, Esther was my hero, and indeed, we were similar. Like her, I was beautiful and doted upon, and like her, I grew up in the shadow of a ruling royal family, since my older brother was the personal physician to the King and Queen of Portugal. Our family was well assimilated into the culture of Lisbon.

Q: Did you grow up thinking you were Christian? How did you find out that you were Jewish?

Gracia Nasi: I absorbed faint Jewish memories from unusual things that we sometimes did at home, and also from stories that my father told us when we were alone and the curtains were drawn. He liked to tell us the story of Queen Esther. We would huddle around my father's feet in early spring as he read from a parchment scroll, and each retelling of Esther's story added a layer of meaning to my Jewish identity. As I grew older, the purpose of my father's repeating her story became clear. Her concealment of her Jewish identity until the right time, together with her courage, spoke to my very own family's determination to keep Jewish customs and traditions alive at the risk of our lives.

Q: So you grew up with a faint inkling that you were not like those around you, that you were actually Jewish.

Gracia Nasi: Yes. Even before we were told of our true heritage, we knew that there was something different about us. For example, we had several names. My Spanish, Catholic name was Beatrice de Luna. Later on, when I began to practice my Judaism more openly, I adopted the Spanish translation of my Hebrew name, Hannah, and became known as Gracia Mendes Nasi.

When I was 18, I married another *converso,* Francisco Mendes. He, too, had a separate Jewish name: Semah Benveniste. His family was one of Spain's oldest and most distinguished Jewish families, excelling in commerce as well as Jewish knowledge. Francisco's father, a rabbi, was the financial advisor to the King of Aragon. Semah's family also fled to Portugal with their sons, Francisco and Diogo, whose Jewish name was Meir. Both boys inherited their father's wisdom and business talents. Their family imported spices and fabrics from the Far East to Western Europe.

Q: How did you meet Francisco? How did you know he was Jewish?

Gracia Nasi: Our marriage was arranged. *Converso* families defied the edicts that we must marry Catholics, and arranged marriages among themselves to ensure that their children would marry Jews.

Q: What was your marriage like?

Gracia Nasi: Francisco and I were very fortunate. We discovered instantly that we were soul mates, and we adored each other. He was handsome, sensitive and wise.

Q: Tell us a little about your husband.

Gracia Nasi: Like me, Francisco came from wealth and privilege, but he was also a learned man, even at a young age. He was known as a *converso* rabbi, which meant that people came to him to seek guidance in their struggle to preserve Jewish law and custom despite the lie that they were forced to live. Francisco also excelled in his family's trading business, and as he worked together with his brother Diogo, the business grew significantly because of a sea route to India that had just been discovered. This important and strategic route opened the port of Lisbon and continental Europe to a thriving trade of spices, fabrics, and jewels. The Mendes family also became known as the Mendes Banking House because of the extensive flow of money in and out of all their European ports of call.

Q: Did you have a Jewish wedding?

Gracia Nasi: Francisco and I were married in 1528. Like most *converso* couples, we had two ceremonies. The night before our very grand and public Catholic wedding, we held a secret Jewish ceremony in our new home. We pledged loyalty to God, to each other, and to our people, and prayed for a future when we could live freely as Jews in a rebuilt Jewish homeland in Israel.

The next day, our Catholic wedding was held in the royal chapel. The Pope's ambassador to Portugal presided. The reception was sumptuous, as befitted a couple from such wealthy families. Precious stones were sewn into my gown, which was made of the finest silk, and each guest was given a strand of rubies. Although it seemed a fairytale wedding, it was bittersweet for devout Jews such as my father and Francisco. In silence, secretly, they prayed to God, asking for understanding and forgiveness.

Q: What happened once you and Francisco started your life together?

Gracia Nasi: Francisco and I were very happy together. He rekindled my Jewish memories as I absorbed his passion and yearning for the restoration of the dignity of the Jewish people. He taught me much about faith, God, and the ethics and morals that Judaism brought to the world. He also taught me about the major role that the Land of Israel held for the Jewish people.

The more Francisco taught me and the more we shared our dreams of being free Jews, the more sadness overcame him at the injustices we had to endure. As his most loyal confidante, I also learned how Francisco used his ships and trading houses to smuggle Jews to safer lands, even as far as Israel.

Q: It sounds as though your husband was a profound influence on your life.

Gracia: He was. My life and education had been centered on Spanish culture, which was all I knew, until I married Francisco. He taught me that Judaism was a treasure that had to be hidden carefully, preserved in secret during the dangerous times that we lived in. Yet at the same time, he acted, moving thousands of Jews to freedom.

Q: Did you and Francisco have children?

Gracia Nasi: Yes. We had a daughter, Ana, whose Jewish name was Reyna – "queen."

Q: That was a brave thing to do. Times were so dangerous for Jews, and your status so uncertain even at the best of times.

Gracia Nasi: Yes, it was. We constantly shifted between the happiness of family, privilege and wealth, and anguish from threats to us and our fellow Jews. We used our fortune to bribe the Church and the government to stave off arrest, torture, public humiliation, death. So many bribes…. I had no idea at the time that this would become the pattern of my life. And then, my world ended.

Q: What happened?

Gracia Nasi: Francisco died suddenly when I was twenty-six. I was devastated, as you may imagine. We had loved each other so much, and we had been married for only eight years. To make matters worse, I had to bury him in a Catholic cemetery. It was 1536. Reyna was an infant then, and life was becoming more dangerous for us with each passing day.

Q: How so?

Gracia Nasi: Since we were being watched closely, it was increasingly difficult to ensure safe passage for Jews in our ships. Francisco's attempts over the last years of his life to bribe the church and the king to stave off edicts of persecution were no longer effective. My nephews, the sons of the royal physician, were similarly unable to deflect hatred towards us, even though outwardly we were faultless Catholics. Diogo, Francisco's brother and business partner, had moved to Antwerp, which was now a major import and banking city on our trading route. I was alone.

Q: Didn't you think of leaving, too?

Gracia Nasi: Of course. Diogo helped me transfer money and much of our property to Antwerp. Then one night I bundled up my little Ana, and I told my sister to dress warmly. I locked the door of our home and set out with as many other *conversos* as I could. My nephew, João Miguez – who would later be known as Don Joseph Nasi, the Duke of Naxos – and his brother met me at the Mendes trading house and we boarded one of our ships, hid inside its hold, which was filled with cargo, and sailed to Antwerp by way of England, where local Mendes trading agents kept us safe. Just as we left, an office of the Inquisition was formally established in Lisbon.

Q: Your timing was perfect.

Gracia Nasi: It was lucky. As I left the shores of Lisbon, I saw hundreds of *conversos* left behind, and my heart wrenched inside me as I realized that they would surely die. Looking towards Europe, I envisioned hundreds of Jewish families brought to safety, allowed to practice Judaism openly once more, without fear, streaming across the continent towards the Promised Land. In the hold of the ship, on my way to Antwerp, I experienced a moment of truth. I knew that I must continue Francisco's legacy and help our people.

Q: What happened then?

Gracia Nasi: Diogo met us in Antwerp. He tried to ease my guilt at having left so many of my fellow Jews behind. Once I was safe, I could have hidden in my beautiful and well-appointed home, but our family's comfort only made me think of all the Jewish parents and children whose fate lay in my hands. I had made my decision on the way, and as soon as we had settled into our new home, I began to act.

Q: How did you begin?

Gracia Nasi: I settled my husband's estate. His will stipulated that Diogo and I be co-executors. He divided his considerable fortune between Diogo and me, and my half ultimately became my daughter's inheritance.

Q: So you and Diogo were now business partners.

Gracia Nasi: Yes. Although we managed an enormous business enterprise, our primary goal was to help as many Jews as possible to escape the Inquisition. We appointed trusted agents in Lisbon to continue hiding them in our ships' holds. We paid these agents handsome sums, as we did in many ports, to secure safe arrival in places in Europe where the Inquisition's presence was not as strong.

Q: When you transferred money, how did you ensure that it reach the intended receiver? It hardly seems that such transfers would have been secure in those days, and with such dangers.

Gracia Nasi: Our agents and couriers were mostly Jews, fellow *conversos* whom we could trust because they too had been saved. From time to time, an agent would abscond with money that had been entrusted to him, but for the most part, our agents were loyal. They worked tirelessly and at great risk to their own safety, using our trading houses and banks as safe routes.

Q: Now that the danger is long past, can you tell us the route?

Gracia Nasi: Yes, now I can. It went mainly through Belgium and Holland, across the Alps into Italy or the Balkans, on to Turkey and finally to Israel. Along that route, agents advised the travelers by providing names and locations of inns whose owners were sympathetic, and they gave minutely detailed instructions on how to proceed safely. At the same time, we continued to bribe government officials everywhere. Our personal messengers not only delivered the bribes and ransom money directly into the hands of the rulers, but received promissory notes in return – documents guaranteeing freedom from persecution that were duly signed, officially sealed, and returned to me.

Q: Were you happy to stay in Antwerp?

Gracia Nasi: For a while, yes. I lived in a beautiful house and was surrounded by the elite of society in the arts and sciences, many of whom were former *conversos*. My home was also visited by the Jews in transit eastward and from one of my doors, I served them hot food and gave them warm clothing before they continued on their way.

But it wasn't long before Antwerp also became threatened by the Inquisition as the King Charles V's emissaries increased pressure to destroy the House of Francis and Diogo Mendes in order to seize our wealth.[3]

Q: The Inquisition was following you once again.

Gracia Nasi: It was searching for any possible way to get its hands on our fortune. Diogo was arrested and charged with practicing Judaism – the formal charge was known as "Judaizing" – helping other *conversos,* and being a disloyal Christian. I paid a large ransom for his release, and luckily was successful. No sooner was

---

[3] Charles V (February 24, 1500–September 21, 1558) was ruler of the Holy Roman Empire from 1519 and, as Charles I of Spain, of the Spanish realms from 1516 until his abdication in 1556. On the eve of his death in 1558, his realm spanned almost four million square kilometers. As the heir of four of Europe's leading dynasties – the Habsburgs of Austria, the Valois of the Burgundy, the Trastamara of the Castile and the House of Aragon – he ruled over extensive domains in Central, Western and Southern Europe, as well as the various Castilian (Spanish) colonies in the Americas and Philippines. He was the son of Philip I of Castile (Philip the Handsome) and Juana of Castile (Joanna the Mad of Castile). His paternal grandparents were the Holy Roman Emperor Maximilian I and Mary of Burgundy, whose daughter Margaret raised him. His maternal grandparents were Ferdinand II of Aragon and Isabella I of Castile, whose marriage had first united their territories into what is now modern Spain, and whose daughter Catherine of Aragon was Queen of England and first wife of Henry VIII. His cousin was Mary I of England, who married his son Philip. Charles's reign constitutes the pinnacle of Habsburg power, when all the family's far flung holdings were united in one hand. After his reign, the realms were split between his descendants, who received the Spanish possession and the Netherlands, and those of his younger brother, who received Austria, Bohemia and Hungary. Aside from this, Charles is best known for his role in the Protestant Reformation and the convocation of the Council of Trent. (Source: Wikipedia online)

146

he free when we heard of Jews being imprisoned in Italy, and we set up a fund there for their release. More of our agents were arrested and tortured until some of them broke and gave information about our routes and strategies. Oppression was mounting.

I was on the brink of convincing Diogo that we should close our business in Antwerp and move to another city in order to rid ourselves of the "veil of Christianity"[4] when the unthinkable happened: he died suddenly. This was a terrible blow to me. It was now 1543, six and a half years since my arrival in Antwerp.

This time I really was alone. It took every bit of strength I possessed not to give up and abandon all responsibilities.

Q: What a tragedy for you.

Gracia Nasi: It was. I still don't know how I managed to keep going. Diogo left half of his estate to me as trustee for his widow – my sister Brianda, whom he had married – and their infant daughter, Gracia. The other half of his estate was an endowment for the needy of Portugal and Belgium. Like his late brother Francisco, Diogo was the epitome of a good Jew in life and in death. In his will were bequests to help those who had been wrongfully imprisoned as he had been, as well as money for orphans and the poor who needed clothes. As the executor of his will, I became what you would call today the CEO of one of the biggest import/export and banking houses in Europe. With Diogo's death, I had to postpone leaving Antwerp, since I now had to look after all our business concerns on my own.

Q: Your strength and skills are impressive. So was your conviction to continue.

Gracia Nasi: I had no choice. I turned to my nephew, Joseph, who had accompanied us out of Portugal and on whom I relied a great deal. A trustworthy, talented, well-grounded young man, he traveled for us a great deal and was willing to accept guidance. Although he enjoyed the benefits of our wealth, he established his

---

[4] Roth, 37.

own trading house and bank in Lyons, France, which had become the center of Europe's silk industry. Our goods moved in high volume from India through Lyons.

When Joseph visited us in Antwerp, he enjoyed our frequent invitations to the palace of the Queen Regent Marie, the representative – and sister – of Charles V. Although I enjoyed them too, I was far more cautious in my relationship with the royal family. I always suspected that their kindness was superficial and that they could turn on us at any time, as we had already witnessed when they held Diogo for ransom.

My suspicion was justified when a shady Old Christian nobleman named Francisco d'Aragon, an illegitimate descendant of the royal family of Aragon who was much older than my daughter, arrived in Antwerp. He was frequently the center of attention at these palace gatherings. Apparently, the purpose of his coming was to investigate new charges against the New Christians.[5] As if all that were not bad enough, he hoped to marry Reyna in order to get his hands on her inheritance. When I discovered that he had already promised a substantial amount of her money to Charles V,[6] I was terrified. I was accustomed to paying bribes and protection money in surety for others, but the possibility of losing my daughter aroused the deepest fear within my soul.

Q: It must have been dreadful for you. What did you do then?

Gracia Nasi: I quickly closed as much of our business in Antwerp as possible, which meant more bribes to the greedy and debt-ridden Charles V to annul yet more charges that he had brought against Diogo even after his death. I transferred most of our assets as pressure mounted to marry Reyna to Francisco d'Aragon. I used every excuse not to accept the Queen Regent's invitations, feigning ill health. However, when I could no longer

---

[5] Roth, 43.
[6] Roth, 43.

avoid meeting with her, I finally told her to her face that I would rather see my daughter dead than married to that man.

Q: She must have been terribly insulted.

Gracia Nasi: I'm afraid she was, but at that point I had no choice. Still, one does not rebuff the Queen Regent without consequences. She took her revenge later on – I had to pay her and her brother still more money.

Q: But you escaped.

Gracia Nasi: Yes, we were lucky enough to get out in time. I packed and organized our household, putting it about that we were traveling to a spa, as was customary for well-to-do families such as mine. But in reality, we left Antwerp for good and went to Venice.

Q: Why did you choose Venice?

Gracia Nasi: Jews could practice their religion in Venice if they lived in a ghetto. They could also pay a special tax to live in the city center but had to live as Christians if they did. We paid the tax so that we could participate in business and cultural activities.[7]

Meanwhile, Joseph remained in Antwerp, using his charm with the royal family to cover our hasty departure. The queen, enraged that I had had the audacity to leave so suddenly, immediately placed the assets we had left behind under embargo, but through his diplomatic efforts – and by adding more money to the royal coffers, of course – Joseph got them released. To my great relief, Joseph also left and joined us in Venice.

Q: What was life like in Venice?

Gracia Nasi: I had no time for learning, which I had so loved doing with my husband. Demands and petitions followed me from every corner of the globe, drawing on my emotional strength. Yet every ducat spent seemed to bring me one step closer to what I

---

[7] According to the history as outlined by Roth.

longed for: a life as a free Jew. I often thought of Esther and kept her story close to my heart to sustain me as I sustained others.

Q: So you kept up with your rescue efforts?

Gracia Nasi: In Venice, the iron vise of the Inquisition was loosened, allowing its inhabitants to enjoy the Renaissance that flourished there. Since Venice was a way-station for Jews who were en route to Turkey and Israel, once again my home was filled with a constant flow of weary and frightened travelers. My own goal was the same as theirs, and I only stayed in Italy as long as I did to further settle business affairs and transfer more assets eastward. In Turkey, the sultan was welcoming Jews and allowing them to practice their faith openly. His kindness did not spring from pure motives either, since he knew that Jews would improve his economy, as the Muslim population, which were now the majority and which had overthrown its previous occupiers, the Byzantine Empire, would not.

An old family friend, Moses Hamon, who was the sultan's physician and a steadfast Jew, eased my way to Turkey. He convinced the sultan that my wealth would be of great benefit to Constantinople.

Q: But you were still in Venice, yes? Please tell us briefly about Venice during the Renaissance.

Gracia Nasi: It was a wonderful place to live. The printing press, which had been invented centuries earlier, was perfected there. For the first time, books were available and the discussions pertaining to them became a large part of the cultural community.

Q: Did your family have peace during that time?

Gracia Nasi: Unfortunately, no. While my family and I enjoyed the colorful life of the city's culture, we also suffered setbacks, including family disputes over the Mendes estate. My sister Brianda claimed that I was mismanaging her portion of the inheritance, and she brought her complaints to the courts. I was imprisoned and separated from my daughter, who was sent to a convent together with Brianda's daughter, my niece. My property was impounded.

The state was happy to be involved because they knew that I would pay a high price for my freedom. Eventually I was freed and reunited with my daughter, and my sister realized how foolish she had been. I forgave her betrayal. We were lucky that time.

After this incident, in 1550, I fled to Ferrara, a city south of Venice, where the Duke was kind enough to allow his Jewish subjects to live openly as Jews. Once more I was lucky because just after we left, the process of evicting all *conversos* from Venice began. I emptied the Venice ghetto by paying for as many safe passages as there were Jews. The Duke of Ferrara was a glimmer of light, and although we were permitted to use our Jewish names and live as Jews, many of us were still fearful and continued to keep our adherence to Judaism a secret.

Q: Did you not enjoy the freedom that the Duke granted?

Gracia Nasi: We felt safer practicing out traditions in our homes. Had I been known as an openly-practicing Jewish woman, this would have compromised my status socially and commercially. I could not allow that to happen as long as our own existence and that of so many others depended on our success in commerce.

Q: How long did you stay in Ferrara?

Gracia Nasi: We lived there for two years. The Duke was an educated man who valued the Jewish contribution not only to commerce, but also to literature and the arts. He had attracted many prominent intellectuals, among them the Modena family, who were known for their scholarly women. Fioretta, whose Hebrew name was Batsheva, was an expert in Torah, Mishnah, Talmud, Midrash, and Kabbalah.[8] The Abarbanel family also lived in Ferrara at this time. I was privileged to know them well and benefit from their worldly wisdom and Torah teachings.

Especially notable was Dona Benvenida Abarbanel, who came from a family of statesmen and philosophers. At a young age, she married Don Isaac Abarbanel's son Samuel, who was considered a

---

[8] *The JPS Guide to Jewish Women,* 111.

giant of Torah.[9] Dona Benvenida shared her husband's qualities. Our families were both successful in the trading business, and we believed in the importance of *tzedakah* – charitable work.

Q: It sounds like you found your soul-sister in Dona Benvenida.

Gracia Nasi: Dona Benvenida had become a teacher in the royal court in Naples, where they had stopped in their exile from Spain. There, thanks to her ability to influence others so positively, Jews were often protected from persecution. When Benvenida's husband died, he left her in full control of the family business – does this sound familiar? – which she expanded while still remaining faithful to charitable endeavors and Jewish learning. Although we seemed to share a similar path in life, we weren't close friends. Sometimes we met at social gatherings, and sometimes we met with others to learn, such as Dona Fioretta Modena, whose knowledge and spirituality were awe-inspiring. These sessions were a refuge from our heavy burdens. But mostly we lived under the pressures of our businesses and the difficulties of maintaining the survival network for the thousands of Jews who were fleeing persecution.

All the bribes and gifts we paid were actually the fulfillment of the Jewish commandment of *pidyon shevuyim* – redeeming captives. Apparently, our ancestor Abraham set the standard when he formed the first Jewish army to fight and rescue his nephew Lot, who had been captured by raiders. If Benvenida's family and mine suffered any loss from rescuing captives, we often said that we had been repaid many times over in spiritual fulfillment.

Q: What else did you do in Ferrara?

Gracia Nasi: I sponsored the printing of the Hebrew Bible into Spanish, which made it more accessible to Jews in our community. The book, which became known as the Ferrara Bible, included a dedication to me by its printer, along with a history of

---

[9] "[A] great in Torah, nobility, and wealth... he had all the traits for the gift of prophecy." Roth, 65.

Israel with promises of hope and redemption to save Jews from despair. It was still available in schools in Portugal hundreds of years later – what you would call the late 1970s.[10]

Q: This all sounds wonderful, but I have a feeling that it didn't last. Am I right?

Gracia Nasi: I'm afraid so. In 1551, when an outbreak of plague in Ferrara was blamed on the Jews, we were evicted en masse. I organized food and clothing for many people, and once more we had to move. My family went back to Venice, where I had the terrifying experience of being arrested once more. This time I was charged with having declared my Judaism in Ferrara. Luckily, word of my arrest reached my powerful friend in Turkey, Dr. Moses Hamon, who quickly negotiated my release. We left Venice and were allowed to go back to Ferrara.

By now, I was busy with plans to leave for Turkey as soon as possible. At the age of forty-four, in the late summer of 1552, I left Ferrara with another entourage of family and fellow Jews whom I listed as servants to the authorities. We made a slow journey to Constantinople, conducting business and securing more safe routes along the way.

Q: How did you reach Turkey?

Gracia Nasi: We traveled down the east coast of the Italian peninsula to the port of Ancona. We then sailed to Ragusa – which is known in your day as Dubrovnik – another beautiful port that saw the passage of significant amounts of our goods. The volume of trade in both ports was extremely high and our goods were often confiscated until I paid for their release. We crossed the Balkans to Salonica, which was so densely Jewish that Jews formed the majority of the population and its harbor was closed on Shabbat![11]

---

[10] Roth, 74.
[11] Roth, 86.

Q: Apparently Salonica, Greece, remained a Jewish center until the 1940s, when the Nazis murdered most of its citizens. Wouldn't it be wonderful if we could tour there together in order to relive the beauty of these places without the fear and foreboding that tormented you then?

Gracia Nasi: I could think of nothing finer!

Now we have reached the spring of 1553, when we arrived in Constantinople in pomp and splendor. With our friends and staff, my daughter, sister, niece and I rode through the streets in "triumphal chariots."[12] Forty armed men, dispatched by the Sultan for extra safety along our route, accompanied us on horseback. To celebrate my freedom, I distributed funds to poor Jews of the city. I cleaved more closely than ever to the memory of Francisco, who would have been so happy and proud to see that day. Indeed, one of the first things I did was to have his remains exhumed from the Catholic cemetery in Lisbon and transported to Jerusalem, where they were given Jewish burial in the Valley of Jehoshaphat. His journey to the Promised Land had ended, while mine had not. I prayed for the peace of his soul, and that I would soon join him in the Promised Land.

Q: How safe did you feel in Turkey?

Gracia Nasi: I did not delude myself, nor did I trust the Sultan's kindness completely. I knew, once again, that we Jews were valued only for what we could contribute to the economy, and that he wanted a piece of my wealth. So I continued to look eastward.

In the meantime, we settled in the beautiful Palace of Belvedere in the suburb of Galata, which our friend Dr. Moses Hamon had chosen for us. Once again, the doors were open. The poor received a meal at one entrance, while businesspeople or petitioners for favors passed through another. I made another fine friend, Esther Kiya, the young widow of a rabbi. She had her own successful business and was generous and also loved to learn. She funded the

---

[12] Roth, 83.

building of homes in the Jewish quarter, as well as the printing of books and the establishment of houses of learning. She herself was so learned that she was often consulted by the Jewish court of Constantinople in matters of divorce.

Q: So once again, all was well.

Gracia Nasi: Yes, once again, in yet another city. What made me happy was the arrival of my nephew Joseph, who settled in Constantinople and helped to consolidate many business concerns. This was when he became known for the first time as Don Joseph Nasi. How proud my brother would have been of him, handsome and successful, especially in the political world. And greater joy came when he married my daughter Reyna.

Reyna and Joseph's life was exciting, because Joseph had befriended the young prince, Selim, the heir to the throne. Joseph became a diplomat with political power that spanned Europe and the Turkish Empire, and in 1566, Sultan Selim made him the Duke of Naxos and the Cyclades. Joseph continued to work with me for the safe passage of Jews, to establish Jewish hospitals, synagogues, and schools in Turkey, and to support the Jewish scholars of our time.

Q: It was then that you made an important land purchase, I believe.

Gracia Nasi: Yes. We bought land in Tiberias from the Sultan, where we established a Jewish settlement and Talmud academy. In this project, I was inspired by Gracia Aboab, who also had fled from Spain via Florence. She had reached Israel more quickly than I and had already founded two rabbinical academies, one in Jerusalem, the other in Safed. Now I had to catch up!

Q: And then, tragedy struck again.

Gracia Nasi: Yes – the horrible events in Ancona.

Throughout my adult life, I had used political and monetary resources to respond to evil. In this last deed, I initiated an offensive aimed at exacting retribution from the Pope himself. He had burned our books and tortured and murdered our people, and we had done all that we could to keep out of his reach. But now, he began to break all the promises that we had bought from him to protect those Jews still in his papal states.

The incident to which I refer became known as the Ancona Boycott. Ancona, the port from which we had sailed, was a point of departure for thousands of ships and travelers. It had become a large Jewish center, boasting many Jewish doctors and scholars, and we based many agents there. We had paid the Pope enormous sums to allow the Jews to live in peace. But in 1555, he broke all the agreements he had made with us and ordered a brutal campaign there. He was angry over the division of the Church by the Protestant movement, and vented his wrath on the Jews. On his orders, the Inquisition jailed and tortured most of the Jews who lived in Ancona, about a hundred in all. In the end, twenty-five Jews were burned at the stake. One of my own agents, Jacob Morro, died in that incident, though we never learned whether he had been executed or died in prison.

Q: How did you respond?

Gracia Nasi: I was furious, and determined to strike at the European economy with the full force of our trading power.

I met with the Sultan and, like Esther before me, I used grace and charm to influence him. I also hinted at potential disastrous consequences to his own trading empire if he would not comply and we were to leave Turkey. In the end, I convinced the Sultan to put an embargo on products and impound all vessels from Ancona in Turkish ports, barring them from unloading, loading, or leaving. We also transferred all our trade from Ancona to the port of Pesaro, to the north, hoping to shut Ancona down completely.

I publicized the tragedy unfolding in Ancona throughout Turkey and implored all Jews to remember we are all a surety for each other. When the Sultan supported my plan, I made sure I had the complete approval of the rabbinic community. Then I proceeded with the embargo.

Q: Were you successful?

Gracia Nasi: Yes. The boycott succeeded for eight months, with harsh penalties for those who violated it.

Q: Was it effective in saving lives?

Gracia Nasi: I like to think that it was, though we will never be completely sure. It infuriated the Church a great deal, which alone gives me satisfaction to think about. But several Turkish rabbis feared that the embargo would endanger Jewish lives even more, so it did not last long. Still, the port of Ancona never saw our trading ships again, nor did it ever return to its former glory. We rescued the Jews who were left in Pesaro. I did what I could.

Q: Your act took a great deal of courage.

Gracia Nasi: I could only hope that the embargo might be a model of resistance for future generations who rise up against oppression.

Q: What would you say to young people today?

Gracia Nasi: I would say: Know your history, and go to Israel where you can experience being a Jew in all dimensions of life. Even with our fortune, our power, our banking house, my family and I were constantly on the run, never able to stay anywhere comfortably or for more than a brief time. You are fortunate to have Israel, as we did not.

Q: You set out for Israel in the end.

Gracia Nasi: Yes. As I approached my fifties, I became very tired. The pressures of politics, diplomacy, travel, business, and family left me drained, so I delegated more responsibilities to Joseph. Tiberias and Jerusalem beckoned[13] – and concerning that, I have something to say. May I?

Q: Of course.

---

[13] It is not known whether Gracia Nasi ever reached Israel. Her burial place is likewise unknown.

Gracia Nasi: You are fortunate to have the State of Israel, and that you no longer have to hide or live a life of wandering. You are fortunate not to be at the mercy of fickle rulers who are kind one moment and cruel the next, who make agreements only to break them when they find it convenient. Have you ever seen Tiberias or Safed? Have you seen Jerusalem? The expulsions that caused us to flee and wander lit a spark of longing in our hearts for a Jewish homeland that was reborn only a little while before your time. While we began to build in Tiberias, we never forgot Jerusalem. Be sure that you do not forget it, either.[14]

---

[14] This interview is based on Roth's narrative.

HENRIETTA SZOLD

HENRIETTA SZOLD was born in 1860 in Baltimore, Maryland. Her father was a rabbi and both father and mother were strong and warm in nature, learned and humanitarian in intellect.[1] Henrietta inherited all of these characteristics, and although she saved thousands of lives, she never saw herself as a hero. Although she had no children of her own, she saved the lives of thousands, both from disease in Israel and from the death chambers of the Holocaust in Europe. A teacher, editor, and meticulous planner, Henrietta Szold had an impeccable eye for detail and an ability to make things happen, but remained humble throughout her life. Her story stands astride two lands, the United States and Israel.

In the late 1800s,[2] Jews began to resettle Israel after approximately eighteen centuries of exile and persecution. They had survived as viable, though scattered, communities throughout the world. When they began to return to Israel, they saw that the country had been laid waste by invasions of successive empires in the eighteen hundred years of Jewish absence. The many occupiers had vied for control of this small, precious strip of land at the crossroads of Africa, Asia, and the West. In the 1800s Jews began to trickle in, mainly from Europe, sensing that it was time to try to reclaim their country. Zionism started to take hold in the minds and communities of European Jews who arrived in Israel in what became known as the First Aliyah, the first immigration wave that carved the path towards the independent modern state.

---

[1] Lowenthal, Marvin. *Henrietta Szold, Life and Letters*. New York: The Viking Press, 1942.

[2] Telushkin, Rabbi Joseph. "Pogrom." In *Jewish Literacy*. New York: William Morrow & Company, 1991, 246–248.

It was to this primitive and fragile Jewish proto-state, known then simply as the *Yishuv* (community) and under Ottoman rule, that Henrietta Szold first arrived from the United States, via Europe and Turkey, on a trip with her mother in 1909 at the age of forty-nine. Her independent spirit combined with her integrity, fierce sense of justice, and the terrible need that she saw in Israel, transformed her life into a heroic one. In Israel, she saw disease, poverty, and lack of basic medical services and supplies. On her return to the United States, she immediately "formulated plans for the medical clean-up of Palestine, utilizing the Zionist women of America"[3] – hence the creation of Hadassah International Organization. It was a brilliant idea. And yet Henrietta Szold never acknowledged her greatness even as she changed the face of Israel.

Between her first trip to Israel in 1909 and her own *aliyah* (immigration) to Israel in 1920, Szold created the Hadassah International Organization and succeeded in making it a partner of the World Zionist Organization to raise the funds that would sustain one of the most significant contributions to world Jewry. She helped ensure the future of Israel by ending suffering and disease through medical and social reforms. Her work didn't stop there; in 1933, at the age of seventy-three, in Israel, she created Youth Aliyah, an organization dedicated to children's' rescue and needs.

When the Jewish Agency was established at the 1929 Zionist Congress in Switzerland to oversee the welfare of Jews worldwide, Szold was appointed a member of its executive. Although Youth Aliyah had been created under the umbrella of the Jewish Agency, Szold knew that Youth Aliyah needed immediate action and, like the children it served, a great deal of attention. Its goals were pressing and could not afford to languish in the red tape of a larger agency. In her political astuteness, she convinced the Agency that Youth Aliyah could be funded by America's Jews. In this way, she brought Youth Aliyah under the auspices of Hadassah, because she

---

[3] *Hadassah WIZO Commemorative Book.* 1993, 37.

knew that Hadassah was committed to action and responsibility and that the appeal in America to save children's lives would succeed. She was right, and Youth Aliyah became not only the lifeline to Israel for thousands of children from Nazi-occupied Europe, but also their guardian in ensuring that they would adjust and thrive in their new land.

In the U.S., Canada, and England, Hadassah attracted hundreds of women forming many chapters that organized fundraising activities. But the organization's credo was also to enrich its members. It revitalized the spirit of Zionism, becoming "the most important mode of Jewish identity and offering (world) Jewry an 'ideology of survival.'"[4] In Hadassah's records, it is written that their "guiding light was service and Jewish learning… an espousal of an idea meant acceptance of responsibility… study and knowledge (were) the bases of action."[5] The women of Hadassah felt empowered and meant business. If Jews in Palestine were in need, Hadassah women would use every ounce of their energy and creativity to raise money for their survival because they understood that a strong Palestine meant greater hope for Jews everywhere.

Hadassah funded medical and social services in Palestine, where disease and poverty were rampant. In its mandate to fund Youth Aliyah, Hadassah brought thousands of Jewish children from Nazi Europe to safety in Haifa, where they were needed to build the homeland. An enormous number of volunteers in the United States, Canada and England, did all this thanks to one woman: Henrietta Szold.

Szold "had two shining threads that ran through all her thinking and planning – one, the child: the other, unity for the scattered

---

[4] *Hadassah WIZO Commemorative Book,* 38.
[5] De Sola Pool, Tamar. "Henrietta Szold." In *Great Jewish Personalities in Modern Times,* edited by Simon Noveck. New York: B'nai B'rith Department of Adult Jewish Education, 1960.

remnant... that make up 'the ingathering of the exiles.'"[6] Today, those threads have been woven into the fabric that is modern Israel. Henrietta Szold gives us her unique perspective.

Q: THANK YOU for agreeing to be interviewed, Ms. Szold.
Henrietta Szold: I am honored to share my story with you.

Q: Would you tell us a little about yourself?
Henrietta Szold: Of course. As you told your readers, I was born in Baltimore in 1860, the eldest of seven sisters. My father, who was a rabbi, taught me Jewish history, ethics and philosophy, as well as a love of human nature. My mother, who was the more practical of my parents, was very methodical and recognized the importance of detail in everything. On Shabbat, our house was full of people: scholars, newly-arrived immigrants from Russia and Europe, friends, anyone in need. The atmosphere was always one of "sympathy and understanding." In fact, our house was open every day of the week.[7]

One of my first memories was going with my parents to meet ships arriving with Jewish immigrants who hoped to start new lives in America. The new arrivals often ate their first meal in their new country in our home. Another early memory is of being hoisted onto my father's shoulder over a sea of people to see a horse-drawn funeral cortege winding through the streets of Washington, and my father later explaining to me who Abraham Lincoln was.[8] My parents cherished the ideals of freedom and human dignity in America. President Lincoln was a hero and his murder was a tragedy for everyone.

Q: Would you say that your upbringing encouraged you to be idealistic?

---

[6] Zeitlin, Rose. *Henrietta Szold: Record of a Life.* New York: The Dial Press, 1952, 209.
[7] *Record of a Life,* 10.
[8] Ibid., 14.

Henrietta Szold: Oh, yes. In my late teens, as a new teacher, I always fretted over whether I was instilling a love of learning in the children as my father had done for me. I also was involved in curriculum development in the Jewish school in his synagogue. I also enjoyed writing, and wrote articles about Jewish life in America.

Q: Did you find that writing took you in a new direction?

Henrietta Szold: It did indeed. By the time I was twenty-eight years old, I was working for the Jewish Publication Society, a new publishing house to encourage Jewish authors and readers. By thirty-three, I had left teaching to become a full-time editor there, and I moved to Philadelphia, where the publisher's office was located.

Q: You couldn't work at home?

Henrietta Szold: Oh, no! We didn't have email or telecommuting then. We had to be in the office to do the work.

Q: And what about the ideals that your father taught you? Did they find any expression in your life at that time?

Henrietta Szold: Definitely. When I was still in Baltimore, I had been involved in an important project: a school for new immigrants.

Q: How did that come about?

Henrietta Szold: In order to answer that, I must explain some of the history of the time. During the 1880s and 1890s, a large wave of Jewish immigrants came from Russia and Eastern Europe. It was clear to everyone that the new arrivals were having difficulty with the language and culture of America, and at risk of becoming the new poor of our country. Although the Jewish population of United States was now nearing one million, many people didn't understand the way of life or the laws of the land. For this reason, they could not get jobs to support themselves.

After many discussions around the dinner table and seeing how difficult it was for new arrivals to become established, I began to teach evening classes at my father's synagogue in English and American society. Since the first groups grew to capacity right away, we started a night school for immigrants with my family's help. We rented space in a school and taught American history and culture, English, and practical skills such as bookkeeping and dressmaking. By 1898, our program had more than five thousand graduates. At that point, the city of Baltimore took over its administration and used it as a model for the education of all new immigrants.

Q: So this was your first experience in taking an idea and giving it form and substance?

Henrietta Szold: I think that this was my first encounter with my own sense that anyone with a good idea can make things happen. My idea was rather simple, but no one was doing it. Talented people who had a great deal to offer their new society were prevented from doing so because of problems that could be easily solved. By teaching them English and basic, marketable skills, we restored their dignity. My parents were proud of me.

Q: So this was the first building block of the foundation from which your life would grow.

Henrietta Szold: I suppose it was. Another part of it was established when my father brought me with him on a trip to Eastern Europe. There, we saw the impoverished villages and neighborhoods from which the immigrants came to America and the persecutions they endured. Millions of Jews were in a precarious state. When I returned home, I joined the early Zionist movement in America, since now I realized more strongly than ever that we desperately needed a homeland in Israel.

Q: What happened next?

Henrietta Szold: I was forty-two years old, living in Philadelphia and working at the publishing house, when my father died. I took my mother in to live with me the following year, and then we moved to New York. I became involved with the Zionist

Organization of America, was still editing, but studying at the new Jewish Theological Seminary.[9] My Zionist activities kept me active socially but I joined yet another group called the Hadassah Study Circle, where we studied Judaism and Zionism together. The purpose of this group, which had fifteen members in New York when I joined in 1907, was to promote Jewish awareness, learning, and the importance of Palestine to Jews. They wrote and distributed educational materials and kept abreast of the political advances of Zionists such as Theodore Herzl and others in Europe. Since the Hadassah Circle's material was often published in the New York newspapers, the public was kept informed about what was happening on the Zionist front.

Q: And then?

Henrietta Szold: In 1909, seeking healing after a devastating heartbreak, I went to Israel with my mother. It was there that I found the mission that I would pursue for the rest of my life.

Although Palestine enjoyed a rich intellectual life, the physical conditions there were deplorable. We saw countless children who suffered from eye diseases and malnutrition. Malaria, typhus and cholera were everywhere. Flies were everywhere and clung to their faces. We saw babies being born in unsanitary, crowded homes, delivered by untrained midwives. In Jerusalem and the outlying colonies, the people were vibrant but suffered from poverty, lack of sanitation, and disease. In Jerusalem alone, there were three physicians for approximately fifty thousand Jews. My mother turned to me and said: "This is your work, Henrietta. This is what your Hadassah Circle should be doing." These were her exact words, and I agreed.

Q: What happened after you returned to New York?

Henrietta Szold: Over the next eleven years, I became a politician, lobbyist, advocate and salesperson. I told the Hadassah

---

[9] The Jewish Theological Seminary, which is the rabbinical school of Conservative Judaism, was established in 1887.

Study Circle what we had seen in Palestine and three years later, on Purim, the first chapter of the new Hadassah organization was formed in New York. Its purpose was to raise funds to send modern medical staff and equipment to Palestine. With the help of a wonderful benefactor who shared our vision, Nathan Strauss, and the women of Hadassah, we sent two nurses to Palestine in 1913. We had arranged for them to start working under the auspices of the Jewish Health Bureau in Jerusalem, which had been set up by another benefactor. The nurses immediately began treating the children's eye diseases and working with a part-time doctor. They also began training women to be midwives and nurses and advised mothers on diet and nutrition. They reached the women by word of mouth and in the soup kitchen they set up at the same time.

Q: It sounds as though your organization was fulfilling an urgent need. I suppose it did not take long to spread throughout the country.

Henrietta Szold: Indeed, it spread quickly. The organization formed the American Zionist Medical Unit, which reached settlements in the north of the country, where malaria was rampant in the great swamp of the Hula Valley, and Tiberias, which had a Jewish community as well. Three years later, the International Zionist Organization asked Hadassah to increase the medical force in Palestine. Once it accepted this challenge, the American Zionist Medical Unit became the Hadassah Medical Organization, and changed the situation in Israel within five years.

Q: Your organization started a nursing school in Jerusalem that exists to this day, correct?

Henrietta Szold: Yes. The nursing school was part of the new Hebrew University and its medical school, which were located on Mount Scopus in Jerusalem. They became a part of the Hadassah Medical Hospital, which served Arab and Jew alike.

Q: Where were you living then? What was your life like?

Henrietta Szold: I moved to Palestine in 1920 when I decided that I needed to be there full-time in order to evaluate and plan the progress of our endeavor. One of the first things I did when I arrived was to transfer the Health and Education Department from the World Zionist Organization in Switzerland to the governing committee in Palestine. In time it became the local Department of Social Welfare. Now we could proceed with establishing a school of social work and to create a plan for working with the population. Today, the Department of Social Welfare is still part of the government of Israel.

Q: You must have been working very hard.

Henrietta Szold: Life in Israel was hectic indeed. Because I was alone, I could focus on my work, and often I worked sixteen-hour days. I often traveled to the United States in order to raise funds and seek volunteers. On one visit to New York, I spoke to local welfare workers and was asked how I could function in so many fields without formal training. I answered, "My work is that of a mother who must watch out for her children's wants and for their future. The people of Palestine are my children, and I feel like the mother who must be on the lookout for symptoms of illnesses and provide against them. My work, like the mother's, comes from the heart."[10] I cannot explain it any better now.

Q: You seem to have had no personal life.

Henrietta Szold: I had one regret in life – that I never had a child of my own. I melted when I saw mothers and children suffering, whether they were Arab or Jewish. After the heartbreak I suffered when the only man I had ever loved married someone else, I never fell in love again, and I had never been in love before I met him. Perhaps it was my fate to be alone so that I could accomplish everything I had to in Israel. Today, single women have children on their own. Perhaps I might have done that if the option had been available to me, but in my day, it was unheard of and would have ruined my reputation.

---

[10] Lowenthal, *Life and Letters.*

Q: You traveled back and forth frequently.

Henrietta Szold: Yes. When I started Hadassah to fund the first medical unit, I also traveled to Montreal and Toronto in Canada.

Q: A close family friend, who is now 104 years old, met you in Toronto when she was a young girl. One evening, she was asked to help out at her aunt's home where a meeting was to take place with a guest speaker. She slipped out of the kitchen to hear you speak about Hadassah and how important a healthy Palestine was for Jews.

Henrietta Szold: Tell me about her.

Q: This friend, Eva Chait, remembers clearly that it was the spirit of your speech that motivated everyone. When she moved to Montreal she became an active life member of Hadassah, hosting, organizing, doing, and donating. My mother, who is also a life member, volunteered in Montreal, as has one of my daughters.

Henrietta Szold: I went to Montreal on that same trip and before I knew it, five new chapters were formed. By 1921, Montreal hosted its first national Canadian convention. These women established the first School of Household Science in Palestine. At this time, they merged with the World Zionist Organization, becoming Hadassah-WIZO.

Q: By that time, you were getting on in years. You had done more than your fair share, and you had earned a rest. Were you considering retirement?

Henrietta Szold: As a matter of fact, I was. But just when I was considering returning to the United States to live out my final years together with my sisters and their families, I received a message from a woman named Recha Freier, who lived in Germany, where the situation for Jews was steadily worsening. Together with her husband, a rabbi, they were trying to get children out of the country to safety. The children were raising money themselves, and in her message to me, Recha proposed moving the children to Palestine.

At first, I could not bear the thought of taking children from their parents and families, and moreover, the needs for the children already in Palestine were greater than we could cope with. But in 1933, when Hitler came to power, Recha's idea seemed crucial. I set up a separate department in the Jewish Agency in Jerusalem and called it Youth Aliyah. Its sole purpose was to bring children to Palestine. Any male or female child in Europe between the ages of fifteen and eighteen willing to build Zion, be a pioneer, work at road building, agriculture, or whatever it took to build a society, was eligible.[11]

Q: And so, just when you had hoped to retire, you went back to work.

Henrietta Szold: I met every boy and girl who came, upon their arrival or soon afterward. During World War II, some of them enlisted with the Palmach in order to return to Europe as underground fighters, hoping to organize and save their fellow Jews. Many of them never returned. By 1947, we had brought twenty-two thousand boys and girls to Palestine, including a large group from Tehran.

Q: May I take the liberty of making another personal comment?

Henrietta Szold: Yes, of course.

Q: I would like to tell you a family story that is a triumph for you. Your life brushed past ours, and we feel the whisper of your spirit whenever we visit our cousin in Jerusalem. You held his hand when Youth Aliyah brought him to Palestine in 1940 as a young boy. He remembers that you visited his group more than once and spoke a few words to each of them. On one occasion, he recalls that you came with a doctor of psychiatry who offered to help them with the grief and fear that they were most probably experiencing over having left their families behind and not knowing their fate.

---

[11] *Record of a Life,* 144.

Henrietta Szold: The children's well-being, on all levels, was extremely important to me. I loved each of them as my own, and I wanted to do everything possible to help them.

Q: Our cousin spent two years on a settlement and then was sent to another for further agricultural training. After several years, he became one of fourteen young men and three young women of Youth Aliyah who founded a new kibbutz, Ein ha-Natziv. He worked twenty-hour days to develop a vegetable crop and managed a small budget with the others to develop income-generating activities, and to construct farm buildings and homes. At night, he shared in guard duty. The kibbutz members had only one telephone and one radio between them, but had eleven rifles to protect themselves from frequent raids from neighboring Arabs.

My cousin's family now numbers sixteen. His children and grandchildren live on a kibbutz about a mile from the one that he helped to establish. Multiply this by each child saved – twenty-two thousand by 1947 – and you, dear Ms. Szold, may be credited with saving three hundred thousand Jews alone, not to mention the lives that you saved with the medical and social services that began when the first Hadassah nurse arrived in Palestine in 1913.

Henrietta Szold: Thank you for telling me this. It gives me great comfort.

You must know that everything we did for the Jews, we did for the Arab population equally. There are no differences when it comes to healing humankind. I regretted not seeing any real initiatives from the Arab leaders to solve the many problems that existed within their own communities, but that never stopped us from offering them treatment and education.

Q: Hadassah Hospital and the Hebrew University today are still universal institutions, and even enemies who enter its doors are treated as friends.

Henrietta Szold: Throughout my eighty-five years, I witnessed so many wonderful changes in Israel, and I am glad to see that in one respect the world doesn't change. Good men and women do noble acts today, as they did long ago. Wise men and women think

170

great thoughts today, as they did long ago. Jews still cling to the ideals that have sustained us since our beginnings as a people. The soul does not change. It only learns to use new and better ways to share peacefully with other souls.

Q: Thank you, dear Ms. Szold.

FOR FURTHER READING

Abrams, Judith Z. *The Women of the Talmud*. New York: Jason Aronson, Rowman & Littlefield, 1992.

Aleichem, Sholem. *Tevye the Dairyman and the Railroad Stories*. New York: Schocken Books, 1987.

Baskin, Judith R. *Jewish Women in Historical Perspective*. Detroit: Wayne State University Press, 1998.

Bialik, Hayyim Nahman, and Yehoshua Hanna Ravnitzky. *The Book of Legends*. New York: Schocken Books, 1992.

Brayer, Menachem M. *The Jewish Woman in Rabbinic Literature*. New Jersey: Ktav, 1986.

Brooks, Andrée Aelion. *The Woman Who Defied Kings: The Life and Times of Dona Gracia Nasi*. St. Paul, MN: Paragon Press, 2002.

De Sola Pool, Tamar. "Henrietta Szold." In *Great Jewish Personalities in Modern Times,* edited by Simon Noveck. New York: B'nai B'rith Department of Adult Jewish Education, 1960.

Deen, Elizabeth. *All the Women of the Bible*. New Jersey: Castle Books, 1955.

Elper, Ora Wiskind, and Susan Handelman, eds. *Torah of the Mothers*. New York/Jerusalem: Urim Publications, 2000.

Finkelstein, Louis. *Akiba: Scholar, Saint and Martyr*. New York: A Temple Book, Atheneum, 1978.

Frankel, Ellen. *The Five Books of Miriam*. San Francisco: Harper San Francisco, 1996.

Frankiel, Tamar. *The Voice of Sarah*. San Francisco: Harper, 1990.

Frankl, Viktor E. *Man's Search for Meaning.* New York: Simon & Shuster, 1959.

Frymer-Kensky, Tikva. *Reading the Women of the Bible.* New York: Schocken Books, 2002.

Ginzberg, Louis. *The Legends of the Jews,* vol. 4. Translated by Henrietta Szold. Philadelphia: The Jewish Publication Society, 1913.

Hammer, Jill. *Sisters at Sinai.* Philadelphia: Jewish Publication Society, 2004.

Kugel, James L. *The Bible As It Was.* Cambridge: The Belknap Press of Harvard University Press, 1997.

Lowenthal, Marvin. *Henrietta Szold: Life and Letters.* New York: The Viking Press, 1942.

Magriso, R.Y. *Yalkut Me'Am Loez: The Torah Anthology.* New York/Jerusalem: Magnum Publishers.

Maimonides. *The Guide of the Perplexed,* vol. 2. Chicago: University of Chicago Press, 1963.

Pogrebin, Letty Cottin. *Deborah, Golda, and Me.* New York: Crown Publishers, 1991.

Rashi: Commentaries on the Pentateuch. Selected and Translated by Chaim Pearl. New York: W.W. Norton & Company, 1970.

Reubeni Foundation. *Chronicles: News of the Past,* vol. 1, no. 5. 1958.

Roth, Cecil. *Dona Gracia of the House of Nasi.* Philadelphia: Jewish Publication Society, 1948.

Sacks, Rabbi Jonathan. *A Letter in the Scroll.* New York: The Free Press, 2000.

Soloveitchik, Rabbi Joseph B. *Fate and Destiny.* New Jersey: Ktav Publishing House, 1992

Soloveitchik, Rabbi Joseph B. *The Halakhic Mind.* New York: Seth Press, 1986.

Steinsaltz, Adin. *Biblical Images.* New York: Basic Books, 1984.

Steinsaltz, Adin. *Opening the Tanya.* San Francisco: Jossey-Bass, 2003.

Steinsaltz, Adin. *The Thirteen-Petalled Rose.* New York: Basic Books, 2006.

Taitz, Emily, Sondra Henry, and Cheryl Tallan. *The JPS Guide to Jewish Women.* Philadelphia: Jewish Publication Society, 2003.

Telushkin, Rabbi Joseph. *Jewish Literacy.* New York: William Morrow & Company, 1991.

The Pentateuch: Translation and Excerpts from the Commentary of Samson Raphael Hirsch. New York: The Judaica Press, 1986.

The Chumash, Stone Edition. New York: Mesorah Publications, Ltd, 1993.

Weissman, Rabbi Moshe. *The Midrash Says.* New York: Benei Yakov Publications, 1980.

Werblowsky, R.J. Zwi, and Geoffrey Wigoder, eds. *Encyclopedia of the Jewish Religion.* New York: Holt, Rinehart, and Winston Inc, 1965.

Wiesel, Elie. *Sages and Dreamers.* New York: Summit Books, 1991.

Zeitlin, Rose. *Henrietta Szold: Record of a Life.* New York: The Dial Press, 1952.

Zornberg, Avivah Gottlieb. *Genesis: The Beginning of Desire.* New York: Doubleday, 1995.

Online resources:

Jewish Agency for Israel, Department of Jewish Zionist Education. www.jafi.org.il/education.

Schneider, Sarah Yehudit. A Still Small Voice: Correspondence
Teaching in Jewish Wisdom. Jerusalem: www.astillsmallvoice.org

Shalom Harman Institute, Jerusalem: www.hartman.org.il

ABOUT THE AUTHOR

ALICE BECKER LEHRER teaches at the David Weissman Institute of the Bronfman Jewish Education Centre in Montreal and has held senior positions in the Montreal Jewish community for many years, including: serving as the President of the Jewish Public Library and founder of its Legacy for Learning committee, chairing the Advisory Committee of the Melton School of Education, co-chairing the Hartman Institute Lay Leadership Global Beit Midrash Seminar Series, and as board member of Kollel Torah Mitzion and Mizrachi Canada. Alice was the founder and president of the private health care company Orthosport, was the editor of *The Canadian Journal of Occupational Therapy*, and has published in the *Canadian Jewish News*. She is the wife of Harold Lehrer, the mother of two daughters and the proud Oma of two grandsons.